It's Mom-and-Pop, *Stupid*

It's Mom-and-Pop, *Stupid*

A Primer for Entrepreneurs
and Middle Managers

Stephen L. Bryant

Expect To Win!

VANTAGE PRESS
New York

FIRST EDITION

All rights reserved, including the right of
reproduction in whole or in part in any form.

Copyright © 2000 by Stephen L. Bryant

Published by Vantage Press, Inc.
516 West 34th Street, New York, New York 10001

Manufactured in the United States of America
ISBN: 0-533-13490-0

Library of Congress Catalog Card No.: 00-90244

0 9 8 7 6 5 4 3 2

This book could never have been written lacking the unsolicited contributions made by all the people I have worked for, and with, during my career. For either good or bad, they all taught me lifelong lessons.

As well, this endeavor would not have reached fruition without the expert assistance of the co-owner of our consulting company, *Concept XI*. Thank you, Pam Kelly, for being my partner and beautiful wife.

The Lasting Fundamental Truth

In the beginning, God created the family business. Attempting to outthink the Almighty, man created the large corporation.

Contents

Introduction   xi

1. What Gets Measured Gets Managed   1
2. Never Hire Consultants unless They Have a Proven Track Record in Your Business   11
3. Shoot Politicians   15
4. Administrators Belong in Junior High Schools   18
5. Mistakes You Can Eat   21
6. Malcolm Baldridge Is Dead   24
7. Establishing Goals Creates Reality   30
8. Home Is Where the Heart Is   34
9. The Tae Kwon Do Connection   40
10. Grow Your Own   46
11. Everybody Has a Bottom Line   51
12. Basic Organizational Skills   60
13. Building Wealth and for Whom   68
14. When to Buy a Business   73
15. When to Sell a Business   81
16. Adapt; Improvise; Overcome   86
17. The Moral Thing   92
18. You Need Old Warhorses and Young Warriors   97
19. Why Most Businesses Fail   102
20. The Three Ps   110
21. The Ten Steve Bryant Country Boy Business Principles   113
22. One-liners with a Punch   119
23. Conclusion   125

Introduction

Several of my friends and business associates have asked many times in faked sincerity and with underlying amusement, "Well, why would you, Steve Bryant, attempt to write a 'how to' business book for the little guy?"

Simple enough answer: "FOR THE MONEY!"

However, I do have a secondary motive of higher integrity. The greatness of this country was founded by mom-and-pop small businesses, and the strength of today's economy continues to rest squarely on the shoulders of the little guy.

We should never forget that the Fortune 500, the S&P, the Dow, mergers, acquisitions, mutual funds, and the world economy once began as children of the small-business owner.

During my wild ride in the carnival known as big business, I have worked for the mom-and-pops, owned my own business, and survived at near the top of three public companies. As I traveled through the free fall of profit and loss, I came to realize there are but two methods of effectively managing a business:

- Big-company approach
- Mom-and-pop approach

I much prefer the latter for the following reasons:

Big-Company Approach (or Feeding the Monster)

Show me a big company and I'll show you an oversize corporate office filled with egotistical, nonproductive, smarter-than-Moses types, inventing work for their own self-importance.

Any of us who have had the great pleasure and responsibility of actually being made accountable for generating sales and profit clearly understand what I'm saying. Case in point:

Hiring a New Corporate Employee

- You will immediately be told that this new person is a specialist and critical to the long-term vision (yeah, right!)
- Within ninety days, the new employee will have invented a series of quite unnecessary reports he must have from operations immediately.
- Within six months, he will have an assistant.
- Within one year, he will have his own department.

I've never known a corporate office that generated top-line growth or enhanced bottom-line improvement. Most often, it's the opposite effect, i.e., operations must feed the monster!

So, what's wrong with the big-company approach?

- Excessive corporate involvement takes the "real" managers away from the reason we are there in the first place: THE CUSTOMER!
- Ideas are never free-flowing, and contrary to the wise CEO who begs for the little guy's input . . . trust me; it don't run uphill! (I believe whoever gets the credit for the suggestion box invention most likely invented the ashtray and toilet flushing system.)

- Strategy is generally fixed and forced to work until it fails and someone other than the CEO gets the ax.
- Politics always rules in large companies. Any good big-company CEO generally maintains, at minimum, two AKs. They're quite easy to find, however. They are the ones with the shiny noses you send all the reports to.
- And the guy at the top is usually the best politician within the corporation, always ready to sacrifice any employee for the good of the stockholders and the safety of his own backside.

To summarize, allow me to share a true experience:

While working for a public company as regional operations Vice President, I was summoned to the Corporate Kingdom for an urgent strategic meeting. No kidding, the company was losing its blue-chip butt, and corporate office represented a cost of 7.5 percent of total revenue! Duh?

The CEO, politically well established and very bright, unfortunately surrounded himself with several AKs. During the meeting he asked what could be done to stop the bleeding. (Actually, the bleeding had already stopped. . . . We were racing toward comatose!)

Being the most honest and possibly the dumbest of the operating types at the meeting, I felt compelled to speak bluntly, always a mistake at the table of Caesar and AKs.

"Well, Mr. President," I said, not really much giving a hoot if the truth would be readily accepted, "I believe it's time we realize that the corporate office only exists to support operations. If we cut our costs dramatically at the top and allow operations to return to profit-driven activities, I believe we can improve dramatically."

The AKs went ballistic and the CEO pretty much told me I should keep my mouth shut. One year later, the CEO resigned on his own accord and 60 percent of the corporate staff were eliminated. I moved up to COO, the company dramatically improved, and eighteen months later we were so darn good that the parent company sold us. The acquiring company already had a COO, so I instantly became unemployed!

C.B.P. Losing the fight is not nearly as painful if you lost it with integrity.

But thankfully, all is not lost. There remains the small-company approach, about which this book is written and to which it is dedicated.

Mom-and-Pop Approach (or Feeding the Family)

The first basic goal of any new mom-and-pop business is to eat. Higher aspirations quickly follow.

What are truly the ingratiating principles that separate the mom-and-pops from the big-company types:

- The small family business focuses on its employees' well-being and the customers' complete satisfaction in, I'd say, a family manner.
- It's not about this month's profit or next week's board room presentation. It's about survival. If one succeeds, all succeed. It's the CEO not only caring but actually knowing the little people who make the business run.
- It's a family atmosphere from top to bottom and bottom to top as well.
- Working together in close proximity to one another's goals, hopes, dreams, and desires enhances the true meaning of the practical principle called teamwork.
- The small-business owner will create trust, honesty, and freedom to display every talent, large or small. The owner must do so to survive.
- The small-business owner most often is never afraid of hiring someone smarter than himself.

I'm quite sure by now you must know that I obviously prefer working for the "little people." But don't be fooled that this study in basic business principles is solely for the benefit of the small-business entrepreneurs. IT IS FOR ANY MANAGER WHO CHOOSES THE RESPONSIBILITY OF LEADERSHIP.

If you follow and apply the twenty basic principles presented here, you cannot and you will not fail.

It's Mom-and-Pop, *Stupid*

1
What Gets Measured Gets Managed

Many years ago, a friend of mine happened to be my boss and part-owner of a fairly large family business generating $12 million in annual revenue. We operated the largest commercial laundry in three states, and the time had come to make a major equipment decision.

The commercial laundry business is labor-intensive, and my boss spent many sleepless nights contemplating the purchase of a German-made washer, costing $1 million. After a great deal of study, he purchased the equipment. He measured labor savings, reductions to water consumption, electrical usage, natural gas reduction, etc. The *ROI* proved to be less than three years.

The important point here is that he determined the necessary ROI *before* this significant purchase, not *after* the investment had been made.

C.B.P. You can never overmanage the numbers, but you should not attempt to micromanage the numbers, either.

As the CEO, owner, COO, or department manager, you should *measure* weekly, thus *manage*, at minimum, the following:

- Sales—new and lost
- All profit and loss categories that represent individually at least 1 percent of sales
- Accounts receivable
- Pricing—new and existing

- Profitability by account

The best method of "measuring to manage," I've found, is to generate a two- or three-page key data report. This information should be in front of you no later than the Tuesday morning following the previous week's activity, and highlighting all the important business numbers relative to *making a profit*!

The collection of data should be generated at the lowest point of activity and developed upward. Measure by the hour, then the day, the week, the month. People who manage from monthly P&Ls are always playing catch-up.

C.B.P. Monday morning quarterbacks never win the game.

C.B.P. Generally speaking, if you wait until someone pulls the trigger before you measure how close you are, you will most likely get shot.

Let's review each category briefly.

Sales—New

The sales rep makes fifteen calls a day, gets three appointments, and closes one account. By week's end, you have seventy-five calls, fifteen appointments, and five closings. Let's say that represents $5,000 in annual revenue, which happens to be the sales rep's quota. There is much more to measure.

No two sales reps are exactly equal, and measuring quotas is not nearly enough. Let's measure. The sales rep actually produced a 20 percent ratio of appointments to calls and a 33 percent ratio of closings to appointments. WHAT GETS MEASURED GETS MANAGED.

Now, if we can increase number of calls per day, obviously, the end result should improve. Maybe, maybe not. But if we improve prospecting techniques and sales presentation performance, just maybe appointment and closing ratios will improve, as will new sales growth. By *measuring the detail*, you can focus on specific areas of improvement, thus creating an overall improvement to the ultimate result.

Sales—Lost

I absolutely go nuts when I speak with a client about business lost and he gives me a percent of sales: "Well, Steve, we're doing great! We've only lost five percent of our base this year."
WHY!?

If you don't know specifically why you're losing business and carefully manage the reasons why, that 5 percent will certainly grow to 10 percent. So then, why do we lose business?

a.	Sales Department	Oversold, undersold, promises not kept
b.	Service Department	Did not respond to customers' needs
c.	Production	Poor quality, late delivery
d.	Financial	Out of business, won't pay, reducing costs, etc.
e.	Competition	Cut price, delivered better product
f.	Act of God	Flood, fire, or divorce

I will guarantee you that a, b, and c are responsible for 75 percent of all lost business and, if you're not measuring this, the department managers responsible sure as heck won't tell you *they* screwed up. They will blame d, e, and f.

Financial losses (d.) are most often due to a poor selling job and not doing the proper credit checks on the front end.

C.B.P. Lazy sales reps make hungry owners.

Competition (e.): You are going to lose some customers to competition no matter how good you are. But if losses to competitors exceed 20 percent of the *real* reasons for losing business, you have much bigger problems.

Act of God? (f.): Certainly His call to make. Replacing lost business is just as costly as adding new, and in some cases more, due to the loss of your business reputation. Measure, then manage why you lost each and every customer.

Profit and Loss Categories

Any business that chooses to operate without a strong budget is destined to failure.

You should start each fiscal year with a detailed budget for every P&L category of 1 percent of sales or more. (If you don't have a P&L, stop reading this book and buy a good one on surviving bankruptcy.)

It takes a lot of work first time through, but the second-year budget will be much easier.

Preparing a Budget

Begin at the lowest point of measurement, i.e., plant labor as the example:

- Productivity of a particular piece of equipment
- Establish reasonable pieces produced per operator hour (consider downtimes, etc.)
- Hourly rate
- Benefits and taxes
- Pieces times hours, times rate, times number of employees
- You now have a plant labor budget

I have always maintained that every employee's productivity

should be measured and often told that was impossible for certain job descriptions. No, it is not!

Two examples of impossible:

A secretary:

Give the secretary three people to work for. When the secretary gets behind, cut back. For nonproductive measurable jobs, *work down* to maximum, not up to.

A janitor:

In the late eighties, I managed a very large plant in Las Vegas, 250,000 square feet of floor space with lots of big equipment, 700 employees, and serious dirt. A very easy place for any good janitor to hide. We devised a cleaning schedule by the hour and square footage with *specific* tasks and times. We also dressed our janitorial staff in red jumpsuits, making it more difficult to blend in and away. We measured and we managed.

Back to budget preparations. Follow the plant labor example for all other P&L categories.

Now each Tuesday morning, with that first hot cup of coffee in hand, you are ready to review, react, and correct. You are prepared to manage your business, not react to it.

Your *key data report* is in front of you.

Category	Week Ending	Budget	Variance	Prior Year
Sales New				
Sales Lost				
Labor				
Utilities				
Supplies				
Etc.				

Develop an immediate correction plan for any variance. You've measured; *now manage.*

Accounts Receivable

If you are fortunate enough to have a cash business, bless your heart and pray for the IRS. If you operate, like most, on a credit basis, realize three very important points.

1. Your first forty-five days of sales will go to A/R LaLa Land, so you must be prepared to finance the first sixty days of operations from cash found elsewhere when you start.
2. Current is ten days, not thirty days.
3. After sixty days, you're in trouble; after ninety days, your money is in serious jeopardy.

Things To Do

- Assign one person the responsibility of collecting data and reporting progress for all collection activity.
- Have that same person call every account over thirty days at month-end close. There should be a definite collection plan established and follow-up for each delinquent customer.
- As the owner or manager, review A/Rs carefully and weekly.
- COD after forty-five days late.
- Discontinue service after sixty days late.
- Never let anyone go beyond ninety days.

Pricing

C.B.P. Always be aware of what your competition is doing, but never be controlled by it.

Pricing your product or service based on competition is, at minimum, foolish.

For example purposes, let's establish an operating pretax profit rate of 20 percent. You must, read my lips, prepare a detailed item profitability before you can reasonably establish pricing schedules and accurate pricing ends up at the profit line.

Is that hard to do? Why, yes, it's hard, but so is losing money!

I have managed or owned:

Commercial laundries
Dry cleaners
Printing company
Commercial janitorial services
Advertising agency
Retail grocery (Kroger)

In every case, it was critical to our successful future that we studied and prepared an item profitability. Some businesses are easier than others, but in every case, this principle is absolute.

How To in Simple Terms

- Cost of raw materials
- Cost to produce labor/utilities/supplies, etc.
- Sales cost
- Service/distribution
- Administrative Overhead

Add in profit, and you have pricing!
Let's make a mousetrap:

Cost of wood and wire	25 cents
Assembly	10 cents
Distribution	5 cents
Administrative Overhead (includes all office costs, administrative salaries, cost of money for inventory, bad debt write-off, etc.	8 cents
	48 cents

I need to sell my mousetrap for 60 cents to generate the 20 percent profit.

Without preparing a detailed item profitability, you are playing a guessing game that you will most likely lose.

Questions

1. The competition is selling the mousetrap for 55 cents! "Then the competition is buying cheaper, producing at a lower cost, or has less overhead than you do."
2. If I sell my mousetrap for 49 cents, I'll at least be contributing to my fixed cost. "Variable accounting will bury you sooner rather than later."

Solutions:

1. Cut cost.
2. Reduce overhead.
3. Decide if growth at a lower profit margin is acceptable.
4. Build a better mousetrap.

5. Develop a better marketing approach.
6. Consider manufacturing rat poison.
7. Invest your money in mutual funds and forget the mousetraps.

C.B.P. Every business that begins with the correct detailed profit-driven pricing structure... eventually ends there as well... profitably.

Profitability by Account

So many times in my career, I have seen and participated in giving all my attention to the "demanding" customer. More times than not, the squeaky wheel was also the least profitable, while the smaller, quiet customers generated maximum profit.

It is imperative that you know the profitability of your customer base, not in total, *but individually.*

If your average profit margin is 10 percent, you obviously have some customers generating 20 percent and some generating 0! You must know which is which.

Growth comes in two ways: new business and price increases. Once you have established an accurate system of determining singular account profitability, you can focus on those accounts that need price adjustments. As well, the account profitability function is every bit as important on the front end as you add new customers.

If your current profit margin is 10 percent, why would you ever add a new customer for anything less than the current profit margin?

Developing correct new pricing and account profitability is fairly simple if you have previously introduced *item profitability.*

In summary, WHAT GETS MEASURED GETS MANAGED.

Please test this principle. Take any area of your business that is currently not effectively measured for a precise and absolute result. Apply a standard and measurable requirement. The results will improve 100 percent of the time.

2

Never Hire Consultants unless They Have a Proven Track Record in Your Business

Did you ever wonder why you can't get a college degree in consulting? If you could, I'm sure it would be a B.S. degree.

C.B.P. If you don't know how to do it and it's of major importance, most likely hiring someone with the necessary talent is a wise decision. Good people never cost you money.

I also realize that in many cases a particular business that is too small or in the start-up mode cannot afford to add the expense for a full-time experienced individual. In that situation, a consultant is the best option.

I personally don't much care for consultants, even though I am one. But, before I decided to take the easy way out and become a consultant guru, I had managed forty-seven operating plants across America, started two new businesses, and been responsible for numerous turnarounds in three major companies within my industry, over twenty-five years. Been there . . . done that!

Most consultants have two things in mind when hired:

1. How do I get this company to give me a second job?
2. How do I pick the brains of the existing team and present the owner with a fancy report that highlights what is already known amongst the troops?

Classic Example

While working for a large international company with sales exceeding $4 billion, I found myself face-to-face with the CEO of the parent corporation. At that time I was the COO of their $100 million uniform rental company in the United States.

He profoundly asked, "What is your primary marketing strategy, Steve?"

I responded, much to the dismay of my British boss, who was standing there shaking like a wet dog, "We pick up five dirty uniforms each week; we clean them and press them. We deliver the product back to the customer with enthusiasm and do so at a fair price. If we do these simple tasks better than our competition, we win. If we don't, we lose."

Needless to say, the big guy did not much care for my brutally simplistic and honest answer. He needed something grander. He longed for a Super Bowl ad campaign. He also failed to realize that our business was not NASA. We were not attempting to put a man on the moon. We were in the dirty laundry business.

Long story short: The big guy employed the services of one of the most prestigious marketing consulting firms in America. After he sent me and nineteen other members of our laundry business to spend a week with the greatest marketing minds in the world, the results were astounding.

Trust me when I tell you that a week of "free thinking and marketing soul-searching" produced the following result.

"The company should focus on delivering the highest-quality uniforms with professional service at a competitive price!" Sounded pretty familiar to me.

This little exercise in marketing and consulting guruism only cost $100,000!

At dinner the final night of our week-long meeting, I addressed the six consultants assigned the task of formally telling me what I already knew. The six individuals were at least MBAs or higher from the very best schools in America.

I presented each member of the group individually a very cheap bottle of Mogan David wine and inquired, "Have any of you ever enjoyed a bottle of the old Mad Dog before?"

In unison, a profound "NO!" A simplistic exercise in you get what you pay for. Unfortunately, this was not the case with our marketing consultant experts. We paid for Dom Pérignon and received a bottle of Mad Dog!

I inquired further, "Have any of you ever made a cold sales call before?"

At least they were honest consultants and again replied in the negative, which caused me to ponder, "How can you develop a marketing strategy if you are void of any real sales experience?"

Case in point? *C.B.P. If you have cattle to rustle, hire a cowboy, not an MBA consultant!*

Several years ago, my big-guy CEO was fired after our $4 billion company became $2 billion. He sued the company for severance. I always wondered if he took a consultant to court with him?

Question: Do I need a consultant?

Answer: Will the return on investment be evident, provable, and deliverable in cash terms in less than one year and ongoing? If yes, hire one.

Selecting a Consultant

- Require résumé with *real* in-the-trenches work experience as a previous manager of something.
- Call last five places where consultant worked.
- Hire consultant for two to five days and give him complete free movement within your organization. *Don't tell him anything;* rather, ask that he review your operation

and make *profit-driven* recommendations. If he can find the problem, most often he can solve it.
- Negotiate a small up-front rate and tie the consultant into a percentage of the overall *real cash* improvement.
- Require on the front end a defined minimum result before the consultant begins.

3
Shoot Politicians

Let's begin by listing those groups of people we trust the least (not necessarily arranged in order of forthrightness):

Used Car Salespeople: Would you hire one to manage your sales department?

Lawyers: Could one help you define an exact and precise business strategy? (Actually, they are the very best at CYA advice giving.)

Psychiatrists: If you're faced with a difficult decision, do you want the truth or an expensive stroll down memory lane?

Politicians: My absolute favorite. Does any real business owner want an AK to always tell him what he wants to hear? Political business animals will always destroy a business and survive to sincerely ask, "Who, me?"

    You must maintain a formal chain of command while also giving your organization a sincere open-door policy. It's a balancing act sometimes, and as the leader, you must be prepared to wear the robe of Solomon on occasion.

    Politicians, for the most part, are not naturally born. They are created and the person at the top can often unconsciously be their creator.

If your organization is truly one dedicated to trust, openness, and free thinking, most soon-to-be politicians will self-destruct.

The road to the top and future advancement for each of your employees must be paved with opportunity borne out of hard work and achievement, not AK activity, BS purification, or stealing the ideas and hard work of others.

Remember, although it helps, you don't always have to like an employee to promote him.

C.B.P. Reward, advancement, and leadership responsibility should only go to the individual that puts money in your pocket rather than accolades in your ear.

I watched football games and drank beer with best buddies. I managed and depended on truthful, dedicated employees. Mixing the two, too often, can help create new politicians. More than once I have fired people I truly cared about, and at the same time I have promoted and rewarded employees that I absolutely detested. The one position that must be void of political aspiration is the position at the top of the heap.

How To Spot Politicians in the Making

- They love to tell you what somebody else has done or said that will not be favorable to your way of thinking.
- They never disagree with you, even when you are dead wrong. (Test that one if you don't believe me.)
- They create adversaries, always weaker than themselves.
- Most will tell you daily of their accomplishments, which more often than not are the achievements of a quieter, good employee.
- They are the ones with the big smiles and shiny noses.

If you spot a developing politician, shoot him before he poisons your organization. There is no cure for the confirmed political animal except elimination.

Absolute Rule: *C.B.P. Show me first. Tell me after.*

4

Administrators Belong in Junior High Schools

C.B.P. A growing business needs action people, not study hall monitors.

In 1992, I joined a British-owned corporation operating a subsidiary business in the United States. The story I am about to tell is true, and the names have been changed to protect the innocent.

My initial job was to save a dying business that had been managed by my boss's secretary. It was a near-death experience.

The business consisted of six operating plants scattered across the country. My predecessor, ex-secretary promoted to division president, had been thoroughly trained in the fine art of being an administrator by the greatest of all administrators, my boss!

Try to picture this: The general manager of the Texas plant was a hardworking, came-up-through-the-ranks individual. He, like most of us, detested working for someone who knew less about the business than his newest employee. On the rare occasion when the ex-secretary, now division president, would visit his plant (with assistant in tow), he developed a game called Just How Dumb Are You Anyway? After working for me several weeks, he shared the rules of the game.

He would graciously stand before a very large commercial laundry *dryer* and explain to the ex-secretary how the *washer* operated. The ex-secretary would smile, ask several meaningless questions, and proceed into the next segment of the game. She would then review several reports that the general manager had never seen before, and he would make up bogus answers. She was, however, an effective administrator!

Sadly enough, it gets worse!

Her boss, who was now my boss since she no longer had my job, trained her to be an administrator. Wasn't gonna happen to me!

"Steve," he told me my first week, "I am not an operational guy. I'm a numbers man. My job is to hire ops people like yourself and administrate the vision."

Please, give me a break! How can anyone administrate anything if he doesn't understand the activity *behind* the numbers? Vision? His vision was simply, "Leave me alone and don't tell me of any problem."

I know this is hard to believe, but trust me when I tell you that the longest meeting I ever had with my boss the administrator was during a session with the Corporate Executive Committee. We spent four hours discussing the menu items for the Christmas party!

Don't get me wrong. This was a very nice man who would have been great working at a bank or government agency. Unfortunately, however, we were in a war and losing.

As the administrator, his hours were from 9:00 A.M. to 4:00 P.M. (on good days). As well, *many* Fridays were "work at home" days, where he believed the atmosphere more conducive to thinking through the problems of the business. (You know I bought that one, don't you?)

When he was at work, the entire morning was consumed with reading the local newspaper and the *Wall Street Journal* front to back.

So what eventually happened to the business? The division presidents reporting to the CEO/administrator started working from 8:55 A.M. to 4:05 P.M. and at home on Fridays.

Sales and profits began a five-year continuous slide, and my boss was forced into early retirement. However, I've been told he's now a successful consultant. There is hope!

So, what's my point? Administrators are never as dangerous as politicians but most often as nonproductive.

Remember, *even a fool does not want to be led by a fool.*

Rules to Follow

- If you are an administrator type, hire an operational type to manage your business and stay out of his way.
- Don't pretend to know if you don't. Take the time to learn what it is you are supposed to manage, or give the control to someone smarter than you.
- All administrative employees—and in any business they are necessary—belong lower rather than higher in the food chain.
- If you don't—with great knowledge and understanding—manage the top line, the bottom line, and all in between, there is rarely anything to administer.
- Don't make your secretary a division president no matter how good her shorthand!

Final thought: *C.B.P. How many really* creative *administrators have you ever known?*

5
Mistakes You Can Eat

Any manager, owner, entrepreneur, or CEO worth his salt has made numerous mistakes and often. The key to survival is not to make the *BIG ONE*.

In the thirty years I have worked as a business owner/manager, I've dug more holes than all the groundhogs in Kentucky. But most often I was the only one that knew the hole existed:

- Don't be afraid of taking risks. But when you find yourself waist-deep in the hole, fill it up quickly before it gets so deep that you need help climbing out, and
- know for certain that in work and life you will find "THE WALL" on special occasions. If you do climb high enough to peek over to the other side and really gut-wrenching fear whispers: "Looks pretty dangerous over there," climb down immediately. For the fearless and stupid, going over the wall is most often void of a return ticket.

Real-Life Story

A second-generation business owner who had been through the school of struggle and hard knocks raised a very large family whilst growing a small company. His first mistake was in not realizing the principle given me by a Chinese family I once had the great honor of working for.

- First generation starts the business.
- Second generation builds the business.
- Third generation destroys it.

Being a good businessman and loving father, he decided to develop businesses for each of his many children—mistake number two.

Side Story

I personally engaged in the great misfortune of hiring two nephews and one son-in-law. All were miserable disappointments and eventually fired, leaving me to look quite the nepotistic fool. Hiring family ain't always the brightest thing you can do, unless you are the rare individual that can *fire a family member* as quickly as anyone else that doesn't produce.

Anyway, the good father began his "build a job" for all the kids endeavor by taking his core business and giving life to new businesses that had a direct relationship and similar applications to the primary core vocation.

Through the first four diversifications, the success rate proved to be 100 percent and the company grew and flourished. Then he made a mistake he could not eat.

The fifth adventure would be the grandest, the biggest, and the most expensive.

Success can be a powerful aphrodisiac. Sometimes it can become one of those unfortunate situations where you've won every battle to date but lose the last one and the war in the process.

This intelligent businessman had probably been too successful. He became blinded and forgot that he previously succeeded due to the simplicity of his offshoot businesses and their similarity to the core business.

With careless abandonment, overconfidence, and little knowledge of the new business, the man mortgaged the other operations and the future of the existing successful family business.

At first the business grew quickly and he believed he had scored the grand slam . . . until the manufacturer he supplied headed south to Mexico. The entire family business was devastated shortly thereafter because the owner made *one mistake he could not eat!*

Mistake-Eating Rules

- Major business decisions are very much like trips to Vegas. Take only the money you can afford to lose.
- You are foolish if you don't have a well-thought-out and formally designed strategic plan for the next three years. Don't venture far from that mapped out road.
- Fearless and stupid sometimes coincide. Yes, you should take chances. Yes, there is the ever-present principle of risk and reward. But never fail to recognize there are always two sides to every decision: it was right or it was a mistake. If it is a "I climbed over the wall decision," odds are in the Power Ball category for winning.
- Don't become gun shy, however, and overconservative, constantly afraid to make a mistake. Just *carefully* examine the shoreline before jumping into the lake.
- Err on the side of being conservative.

Never forget: You can always tell the pioneers by the arrows in their backs.

6
Malcolm Baldridge Is Dead

If I had:

- $10 for every quality statement I have ever heard,
- $50 for every quality book I've been forced to read, and
- $100 for every quality "expert" encountered . . .

I would not be writing this book or doing the consultant tango. I'd be rich and playing golf every day!

If *you* or *your* employees have to embrace quality statements, read quality books, or dreamingly listen to quality expert propaganda, you really don't belong in business. Maybe a job at HUD would better suit your talents.

Let's try a few "quality statements" I've dealt with:

"One hundred percent right, one hundred percent of the time!" (Only if you're God.)
"We do it right the first time!" (Which means they don't count the second or third time.)
"Quality is an all-the-time thing!" (Except when the machine breaks, we're on overtime, or John didn't show up for work today.)

Who's kidding who?
I've owned seven Mercedes, four BMWs, two Jags, and eve-

rything in between. Why is it all gave me a fantastic Roadside Assistance Program? Stuff breaks, and it ain't a perfect world.

Quality starts with *the customer!* It is demanded by, and levels established through, what the customer perceives and requires. There is no need to exceed those expectations, and you rarely will, but there is every need to meet them.

C.B.P. Quality can be as much perception as reality.

True Story (I Amaze Myself Sometimes When I Think about Some of the Professional Clowns I've Been Forced to Fight through Attempting to Make a Profit.)

Our $100 million company, after several years of dramatic growth and profit gain, became quality-focused.

What I find humorous here is that we were so bogusly infatuated with our own genius that we supposed our competition had never heard the word *quality.* Anyway . . . our company hired a "quality expert" after he attended a "quality college." Are you laughing yet? Within ninety days, this quality genius employed two assistants. Within six months, his quality program cost reached 1 percent of total company sales.

Don't get me wrong; we got some great stuff. T-shirts, hats, pins, and the acrylic triangle that pointed to the pyramid of ultimate quality . . . or, in my opinion, ultimate foolishness.

We spent weeks in meetings during the initial setup. We had teams, team leaders, and prizes like you get at the state fair. All the while, our business retention slowly eroded along with our profitability.

Now this gets really hysterical. We were a labor-intensive business, paying just above minimum wage, in war zone neighborhoods. Our average plant turnover ranged between 200 and 300 percent. It took twelve weeks for each employee to finalize his "quality training." Quality school graduation day was a lonely place to be!

I'm sure today that there exist ex–short-term employees in jails across America that have been semi-quality-trained due to the efforts of our "quality expert."

I must admit that God only gave me an average IQ. But I praise Him gratefully for a truckload of common sense. Anyway, two days after I became the COO of the company, the "quality expert" and his two assistants became government statistics.

Please don't misunderstand my point. *Quality is essential,* and lack of it will for sure put you out of business. But you know (or at least you better know) the needs of your customers. Focus on and react to those needs. You do not need a quality statement, quality book, or quality expert. You just need to understand the customers' requirements and instill the importance of same within the minds and good efforts of your employees.

Oversimplification? Ain't it always?

Quality How-Tos

- IT STARTS AT THE TOP!!!

    * You must set the standards and enforce them.
    * You cannot accept a sliding scale on quality standards.
    * You should know explicitly what the customer demands.

- Every employee should have a training period. If they don't, you've already screwed up, and their chance of success is vastly diminished. First step of training is the quality installment. The new employee must know that before productivity comes quality.

C.B.P. Do it good first . . . fast second.

- Quality focus requirements are for <u>everyone</u> in your organization:

  * Plant/production
  * Service/distribution
  * Sales/marketing
  * Administrative, i.e., billing, A/R collection, how we answer the phone. (How many times have you been turned off at a company by the way the receptionist answered the phone?)

- Develop an in-house quality, team, random inspection system.
- Each week by Friday's end, a member of each department or area of responsibility <u>must</u> complete the weekly quality checklist. This, of course, includes you!
- Utilize a simple 1–10 rating system, 10 being the best.
- Composite scoring
- Recap areas of concern with all concerned.
- Focus on inspection problems found and correct them.
- Establish a rule of 95 percent and work up.

How Would It Work?

Simple. *You* complete the checklist Monday; a member of sales, Tuesday; production member, Wednesday; service on Thursday; office, Friday.

Now I'll promise service will rate production somewhere around a 5, production will give service a 5, and sales will give them both a 4. That's why you get to be the leader and your quality checklist supersedes them all!

All joking aside, the beginning process will be a learning exercise and quality standards will self-develop and become universally accepted by the group under your brilliant leadership or dictatorship . . . whichever "ship" floats best.

C.B.P. You should never lose a customer to poor quality.

If you are *measuring to manage,* you will know that and thus begin a real quality in-house program.

Remember, QUALITY STARTS AND ENDS WITH YOU! You are the expert, the book, the statement. And if you are a focused effective leader, your employees will eagerly follow your example.

Weekly Quality Checklist

WEELLY QUALITY CHECKLIST

Day:_____   Week:_____

Person Inspecting:_____
Department: _____

Inspection Team	Rating	Comments
Production Quality		
Assembly		
Loading		
Plant Cleanliness		
Equipment Cleanliness		
Two Customer Calls		
Receptionist		
Employee Appearance		
Etc.		
Etc.		
Etc.		

GENERAL COMMENTS:_____
_____
_____
_____

Obviously, every business is unique as would be the quality checklist format.

7
Establishing Goals Creates Reality

Dreams are for children
Wishes are for fools
Prayers are for God

If you believe goal setting is about dreams, wishes, and prayers, you are childish, foolish, and not well founded in the Scriptures.
    Goals are the beginning of the process that leads to:

Realistic goal setting
Financial review and cash requirement arrangements
Strategic planning
Budgets
Personnel development
P&L accomplishment
Realized result leading to . . .

    <u>lots of money</u> so you can build dreams for your children, fulfill your spouse's every wish, and give a bunch to God for not allowing you to act like a kid or a fool.
    Plus, setting goals is always fun, yet not nearly as satisfying as the accomplishment of goals.

Case in Point

I recently became acquainted with a man whose three young teenage sons belong to the small country church my wife and I joyfully attend. I was told that he had struggled with finding gainful employment and was now attempting to start a lawn care business. Believing in helping others, I offered him my lawn to mulch, and my consulting genius at no charge, hoping, of course, that the latter would be of greater significance.

He began by: "I'm building [dreaming] this business for my children. I will need [wishing] at least twenty customers to begin. I don't have any money [praying]. I lent him seed money, so at least praying worked for him.

Classic example of the old song "Wishin' and Hopin' and Hopin' and Prayin'." Of course, that was a love gone south song, and so was my new friend's business plan.

So what advice did I give him? First of all, I took away the immediate focus of his strong desire to build a business for the three teenage boys and <u>SET THE GOAL</u> of finding twenty beginning customers before any other consideration.

You know, I'd venture to say that every company, large or small, has goals. As well, we most surely all, as individuals, aspire to some goal, be it great or insignificant. The problem, however, always comes back to: Is it really a goal or a wish and a prayer?

Revert back to chapter 1: "What Gets Measured Gets Managed." Once goals are established, <u>they must also be measured</u>, so they can be managed, so they can be achieved.

It is the first element of building a successful business. You set the goal based on your long-term vision and work backward; i.e., I want a $10 million business in five years:

- What are the cash flow requirements?
- Where are the people I'll need?
- I must prepare a detailed budget.

- How do I strategically get there?

Let's run through the procedure after the goal (vision) is established and you've thought through the process:

1. <u>Goal:</u> My goal is to build a $1 million business in twelve months.
2. <u>Finance:</u> I have developed a hard asset requirement and operating cash flow spread sheet based on a conservative sales growth expectation. I go to the bank or SBA or see if Steve Bryant will lend me the money because he recently became rich and famous from selling his business book. Someone with loanable money accepts the forecast.
3. <u>Strategic Plan:</u> Develop sales and marketing approach, method of producing the end result and delivery to the customer.
4. <u>Budgets:</u> Simple. Sales required, cost associated with the sales, debts paid, cash (hopefully) remaining.
5. <u>Personnel:</u> Hire the people necessary to see the budget reach fruition.
6. <u>P&L Statement:</u> The detailed measurement tool necessary to properly manage your business.

Easy enough to do. We start with goal setting, and we move forward by "goal management."

- Daily flows into . . .
- Weekly flows into . . .
- Monthly goals

C.B.P. Short-term goal achievement will always chase down long-term goal reality.

To achieve my goal of $1 million annually, I must secure

$3,846 this Monday. I detail that number in my <u>Monday Goal Achievement</u> action plan.

- If you don't achieve it in eight hours, try it in twelve hours.
- Always attempt to meet your daily goal by early afternoon.
- Always attempt to accomplish your weekly goal by Wednesday night.
- Always attempt to accomplish your monthly goal by the end of the third week.

C.B.P. Catch-up is a dirty word and usually the medal worn by the loser.

C.B.P. If you overachieve early . . . you'll continue to overachieve.

If you fail to achieve your Monday goals and carry them into Tuesday, most often you'll be at least two days behind by Friday and at least a week behind at month end. By midyear, your goal will be reduced to $500,000 per year and the bank will wish you had really borrowed the money from me.

C.B.P. Simple Lesson: Be a sprinter, even if the race is a minimarathon. I'd much prefer being tired and chased to having lots of energy and running last.

8
Home Is Where the Heart Is

C.B.P. Morality isn't just for Sundays.

The golden rule is, in my opinion, the most important principle you can apply to a successfully managed company.

Do unto others as you would have them do unto you.

—Jesus

Pretty good advice, huh!

Building a family business isn't a business where the owners and management all have the same last name. It's creating an atmosphere of hope, an environment of caring about each other, instilling the reality of *you belong to this family* for all employees.

As well, it's developing the same closeness with the customers and with your suppliers.

Think about it.

The Perfect Business

- Each and every employee knows that his well-being is paramount in your mind. They know that if they face a problem with their job, family, or finances, you will be there to help them get through it.
- Each and every customer *believes* he is genuinely receiv-

ing a value for the money he spends with you. Do you have any customers that call just to chat? You should. Customers that feel like they are part of your family business rarely quit, seldom become overly price-sensitive, and most often reject sales efforts from your competition.
- Build a trusting relationship with your suppliers. Many times, my vendors "floated" the growth of my companies. If they trust and believe in you, they can be a tremendous asset.

A family business? Must consist of happy employees, faithful customers, and trusting suppliers. It is *your responsibility* to build those relationships.

Examples

As general manager for a medium-size company in the early eighties, I became increasingly angry with my service manager. It irritates me to no end to have a manager who treats a fellow employee (always subordinate) like a preschool child. Such managers are most often known as purebred AHs.

In this case, we had a route driver that was highly intelligent and totally void of any common sense. He was always the last one to return every day, and attempting to do his paperwork became almost an insurmountable task for him. All that aside, the customers *loved* him and he never lost any business. He had six children, and each evening his wife and a car full of kids would show up at work to pick him up—they only had one car, and his wife needed it to deliver papers prior to retrieving her husband from work.

Now good old Willie (my routeman) had other problems to deal with. To start with, he was bald and wore a wig that looked like it could have doubled as a dust mop. He maintained maybe six good teeth and was stricken with a terrible skin disease.

Here's a guy with some serious physical problems, no money, and a VW filled with kids. Yet this hardworking father of six always had a smile on his face and a kind word for everyone. Maybe that's why the customers loved him, and I must admit it's the reason I loved him also.

My office was located within hearing range of the route drivers' room. *Every day* I would sit in my office and listen to the AH service manager cuss and belittle Willie. I finally told this manager if he ever cursed this poor man again, I would fire his butt! Several days later, it began anew: "You stupid, dumb SOB," etc. etc.

I walked my service manager to Personnel and discharged him. It was a tough thing to do, especially since the guy had been with the company twenty-six years. But no one will ever work for me and abuse other human beings.

Two days later, Willie came into my office and thanked me. He said his life had been dramatically changed because I got rid of his tormentor. Wherever he's at, I hope Willie is happy.

While managing another similar operation in New Haven, Connecticut, I became frustrated with our high turnover in the route delivery department. Up to this point, I always allowed my assistant and the service manager to hire all our service drivers, but with the turnover, I deemed it necessary to join the selection process. This did not make my assistant and service manager particularly happy, but I liked it.

The new procedures would be that as a team of three we would review all applicants and hire by majority rule. I'll never forget the very first applicant.

My assistant, a really funny guy, waltzed into my office to announce the first new potential driver was waiting to be interviewed. He said, "The service manager and I believe you should be the first one to talk to this guy." He smiled one of those "I got ya" smiles. I agreed to be the first interviewer in the selection process, and my assistant failed to mention that the new potential employee had just arrived on a big chopped Harley.

The new man entered my office. He had huge muscles from his ears to his toes and a long ponytail and was blind in one eye. He told me of his struggles in life, the many mistakes he'd made, how he lost his left eye in Vietnam, and *begged* me to give him a chance.

Being an ex–Marine Vietnam vet myself, I decided to hire the guy on the spot. He would start the following Monday.

I then called my assistant and service manager into my office. "Remember what I told you about our new selection process?" They responded in the affirmative. "Well, in this case, I changed the rules."

Service manager: "Do you know this guy is blind in one eye?"

Me: "Yes, he lost his eye in Vietnam."

Service manager: "How could you hire a one-eyed route driver?"

Me: "Does that really concern you? After all, he does drive a Harley pretty good."

Service manager: "How do you suppose he will be able to back his truck to the dock every night if he can't see in the driver's side mirror?"

Me: "Well, if that's the only problem you have, I will instruct him to pull in the yard with his truck, beep the horn, and *you* can park it for him!"

Several weeks later, we strongly suspected a theft problem on the routes. I privately met with my new very tough routeman and informed him of my problem. I said that I did not wish him to become the company rat, but I would appreciate his attention to the problem. Trust me when I tell you that the other route guys respected and feared my Vietnam vet new hiree. The stealing stopped almost immediately. Because I cared . . . *he cared!*

So what's my point? *Always* walk in your employees' shoes, just a while. Be kind; be fair; be understanding. I can promise you if you do and are, the employees will take care of you and your business.

On the other side of the coin, if you believe your business is a kingdom with you upon the throne, whilst peons labor solely for your benefit, you, my friend, will be screwed "royally."

Show me an owner or manager that doesn't build a family atmosphere and I'll show you:

- Higher workers' comp claims
- EEOC problems
- Greater absenteeism
- Stealing
- Customer retention problems

So what should you do?

1. Pay fairly.
2. Provide family benefits.
3. Talk to and search out the dreams and aspirations of your employees; then do something about them.
4. Help your employees financially (with restrictions, of course).
5. Get to know their families.
6. Always offer picnics, Christmas parties, sports team sponsorships, etc.
7. Tell your employees about *your* dreams and aspirations and how they can help you reach your goals.
8. Do unto others . . .

Twenty-one years ago, I promoted a young black man when no one else seemed inclined to give him a shot. Several years later, he honored me greatly when he asked me to be the godfather of his first child. Two weeks ago, he called me out of the clear blue sky.

He now owns his own business and is interested in my consulting services.

C.B.P. The good things you do from your heart for people will always come back . . . and so will the bad things.

9

The Tae Kwon Do Connection

As I sit at my home office desk in front of the huge window overlooking Barren Lake, I am at peace. Being a realist, I clearly understand that getting a business book published is near impossible, although I do find comfort in the fact that many people purchased the book *Mean Business*. I consider that particular book to be "Darth Vader" reading and hope that I can provide the opposing view. Therefore, my book should be published for no other reason than *fair play!*

If this book is never published, so what! At least I've enjoyed reminiscing about all the absurd, lunatic, idiotic people called managers I've been forced to deal with. The following example is clear evidence of just how stupid, well educated, I-am-in-charge, could-not-manage-a-flea-circus people can get.

Mission Statement Stupidity

I believe that for the most part, mission statements are OK, if not wholly unnecessary. I mean for goodness' sake, do you have to remind yourself what you believe in? Mission statements are generally for the CEO, board of directors, and annual reports. But if you have a burning desire to develop your very own mission statement, *please* do so in three sentences or less, much preferring one sentence. In any case, mission statements are generally harmless, feel-good, warm and fuzzy things anyway.

Great Mission Statements

- JUST DO IT
- IT CAN BE DONE
- TEAMWORK WORKS
- ADAPT; IMPROVISE; OVERCOME
- EVERY NO IS A MAYBE; EVERY MAYBE IS A YES

OK then, you want bigger? Do you need warm and fuzzy? Does the customer base cry out for *your* mission statement? Well, go ahead and knock yourself out. Write a poetic, dramatic, soul-searching mission statement. Hang it on every wall and carry it in your wallet next to the picture of your spouse that you never look at, either. Now you'll be happy!

Best Stupid Mission Statement Story

Five years ago, my boss the administrator (remember him from chapter 4?) selected early retirement. Definition of early retirement: "quit, got the ax, or took what they gave you to leave."

His replacement came out of our group of six division presidents and basically got the job in the circumstance of default. Now this guy was pure politician!

The business had lost ground considerably under the watchful eye of the administrator. What could be done to stop the slide, no doubt, would be the first order of business for our new CEO . . . NOT!!

He believed we needed "A Mission Statement"! It does get worse. Not only did we need the old rah-rah; we needed outside consultants to help us dummies develop it. The consultants attended college with the CEO, so the bonding process was not necessary. Now, guess what the names were of the two consultants? DICK AND JANE! I swear to you that is the truth and, I thought, quite apropos.

Here our company sits as profoundly evident as the *Titanic* after the iceberg, and we are about the task of rearranging the deck chairs.

Now, any good mission statement development activity must have three elements:

1. Group participation—which is always a joke since the boys at the top already know what they want to hear and just brought you along to pretend you had input.
2. Flip charts.
3. Consultants that have "real" BS degrees.

All of the above was put in motion under the expert guidance of Dick and Jane, the flip chart gurus.

OK then, how many people does it take to develop a really good mission statement? In our case, approximately fifty.

This exercise lasted four days, with the not really necessary involvement of the fifty company dummies and several weeks of fine-tuning by Dick and Jane.

"Look, Spot, look! See Dick and Jane flip the chart."

Of course, any good mission statement development session must have:

- Teams
- Team leaders
- Additional flip charts and the five-pack color Magic Marker sets

All this in place, we started the mission statement–finding

adventure. It was embarrassing to watch the foolish follow the fools.

We broke off in teams. I refused the team leader position and tried my best not to laugh at the ridiculous spectacle I found myself not wanting to be in. We did the old free-thinking stuff. We talked; we dreamed; we drew a lot of flip chart pictures to envision inner thought conversion to profound mission statement.

Of course, all our fourth-grade flip chart drawings had to be taped along the walls of the very big meeting room. Off the subject a bit, but what would a consultant do without flip chart paper, Magic Markers, and Scotch tape?

The winning picture in my own mind came from our elder Las Vegas Division president. It was a big bus full of people, with huge eaglelike wings carrying the bus skyward. *Absolutely brilliant,* I mused, and contemplated the inner-self mission statement meaning of this profound picture of creative genius.

What could it mean? Maybe . . . "This is the bus from *One Flew over the Cuckoo's Nest.* The driver is our CEO, and the bus is flying away to the funny farm because we are all a bunch of nuts not capable of managing a business." It was pretty close to reality.

Let's get to the Tae Kwon Do experience. After several days of preschool artwork and younger-than-that discussions, there seemed to be no end in sight and mission statement development an elusive endeavor.

However, my mind activated by this unbelievable and exciting challenge, I recalled the tenets of Tae Kwon Do:

- Courtesy
- Integrity
- Perseverance
- Self-control
- Indomitable spirit

Both my wife and I had recently earned our black belts from

Master Kim, the ninth-degree Olympic coach. I thought, *This is it!* A real kick butt mission statement!

I slowly proceeded to Dick and Jane's flip chart and wrote the five tenets in bold letters. They liked them! The CEO smiled broadly, my peers applauded, and I knew instantly they didn't know that I thought the whole thing was a joke.

Long story short, we eventually received a very large package via UPS at my office. Our mission statement had grown to FIVE PARAGRAPHS, all of which were built around the tenets of Tae Kwon Do. Unbelievable!

Now we have huge laminated posters, smaller frameable types, and, of course, the smaller version for your wallet. I thought about two of our green card employees in Mercedes, Texas. I could picture Phillipe and Juan sitting at the little Spanish bar close to our plant, sipping leisurely on their long-neck Miller Lites. "Hey, Juan, can I see your mission statement? Mine got lost in the washing machine!" I threw the whole lot of mission statement stuff in the dumpster, and the CEO was fired in six months. I guess his final mission statement was back to simplicity. . . . Adios!

So, after this rambling story of idiotic mission statement development, what's my point? Simply put, the tenets of Tae Kwon Do are, in fact, the best mission statement you could ever have. Think about it. Can you honestly run your business and manage your people by sincerely believing in and applying these beautiful words that encompass the heart, mind, and soul of real leadership?

1. Courtesy
2. Integrity
3. Perseverance
4. Self-control
5. Indomitable spirit

If you believe and apply these five words, success will be yours readily. But do it in action, not in posters collecting wall dust.

10
Grow Your Own

Your first inclination might well be to ponder the statement "Grow Your Own" and quickly convert that statement to a question: Grow your own . . . what? Tomatoes? Potatoes (Dan Quayle spelling)? Or maybe Grow your own pot (of which I never inhaled)? But the simple meaning is paramount to your long-term success.

Grow your own *key people* for maximum growth of your company ten years from now.

Case in Point

In 1974 I joined a family business with annual sales of $10 million. The business was owned by an extremely conservative elderly man. He was the second generation in the family business and brought his son-in-law into the company to eventually assume responsibility for all operations. This I considered to be one of the few smart things I witnessed the old man do in the five years I worked for the company.

Now, follow this scenario carefully.

The owner believed in the "old school" principle that loyalty is beyond any and all other qualities in an employee. I agree that loyalty is important, but little things like intelligence, creativity, and business skills should play equally in the determination of an employee's net worth.

The old man, however, did not much care for the "other skills," just being real loyal! I watched him create a lot of rats and AKs in the process.

Now he employed several key employees that crawled below his feet and maintained supreme status within the company, i.e.:

- The superintendent of the garage: He watched every gallon of gas pumped from the company tank. He counted every spark plug. He ratted readily on everyone that put a one-inch scratch on a company car that <u>began</u> as junk. He relished his position of King Rat, and the old man crowned him keeper of the snow tires.
- Director of personnel: I doubt this poor old guy could even spell <u>personnel</u> or, better yet, <u>potatoe</u>! His job was to run police checks on everyone, keep the old man's upstairs secret office stocked with booze, and listen through office walls. I guess you could say he was the company spy.
- Director of purchasing: The brain-deadest of the group.

Picture this. Each of these key employees was an officer of the company. Now that I think about it, so was I! But I didn't hold the prestige of these three, as was evident by the old man always calling me . . . "Boy." Now every month we would have a two-hour officers' meeting, which consisted of continuous ratting and spy reporting. We were also paid monthly, and the director of personnel would present our earnings as one might expect a hardened farmer to compensate his migrant workers. Every, and I mean every, month at the officers' meeting, the director of purchasing would proudly attend wearing his white plastic shoes and shiny white, thick linoleum belt. I never figured out why he did not attire himself so gloriously any other day of the month. But I do know Elvis would have killed for the belt and plastic shoes.

So what's the point, Steve?

The point is, the old man did in fact grow his own, so there obviously is a right way and a wrong way to approach this basic principle.

Whatever happened to the "ready to die" loyal employees the old man spent years developing?

<u>Director of purchasing</u> was fired after the old man went to Laundry Heaven and purchased a small liquor store that quickly went bust.

<u>Director of personnel</u> died of a heart attack <u>in</u> the old man's office. I've often wondered if he might have been in the rumor-telling process and the story was just too big for his ailing heart.

<u>Garage superintendent</u>—drawing social security and still praising the old man for his $250-a-month pension.

Now, let's flip the coin:

The son-in-law, a Princeton graduate and holder of an MBA degree, searched for and carefully hired people that could grow far beyond current needs. He looked for and encouraged creativity. In doing so, he developed existing talent and prepared for the future knowing that it would be:

C.B.P. The quality of the people hired today will drive the company's success for tomorrow.

Because of his foresight, the following has happened in the past twenty-five years. Keep in mind this was a small local company, servicing a sixty-mile-radius market.

- Three of his hirees are now millionaires.
- One has written this book.
- Four became regional vice presidents for larger public companies.
- Two became CEOs for larger public companies.
- Seven became general managers for larger public companies.

A tremendous testimonial to one man that knew the critical importance of: **GROW YOUR OWN!**

The Grow-Your-Own Approach

- Go back to chapter 7, *"Establishing Goals Creates Reality."*
- If you have not already established goals, developed a long-term strategy, determined future people needs . . . STOP! Maybe *you* are smoking some grow-your-own pot and consider long-term people planning as a kind of "WOW THING!" Or maybe becoming a potato farmer is a better alternative for you than running a successful business.
- However, if you were smart enough to buy this book, I'm betting you have indeed:

    * Established the vision (long-term goals)
    * Developed the strategy
    * Determined the future people needs

- Look around at your entire organization:

    * Interview *every* employee and determine their long-term aspirations.
    * Draw out organizational structures for: 1 year, 3 years, and 5 years
    * Place the people you now employ in the appropriate slots for the one-, three- and five-year structural needs.
    * Write a job description for each key position.
    * Use formal testing and profiling to help you deter-

mine the overall talent and ability of those employees currently on board.
   * Select those existing employees that can grow into your future needs.
   * Develop a training and development program for each key employee.

- YOU WILL NOT, READ MY LIPS, YOU WILL NOT HAVE EVERYONE ON BOARD TO MEET YOUR LONG-TERM PEOPLE NEEDS!

   * Budget and schedule the hiring of future-need employees.
   * A college degree *is important today,* but a solid, successful track record is equal and sometimes better.
   * OJT is a must and a building to the position process.
   * Present a challenge to the new employee in every phase of his OJT development.
   * Let him see your long-term organization plans.
   * Decide where the new hiree will help you most five years from now, and develop that employee accordingly.

C.B.P. If an employee fails to reach his maximum realistic potential, 80 percent of the time it is because you failed to develop him.

11
Everybody Has a Bottom Line

In chapter 1, I illustrated my past experience story, how my previous boss agonized over the purchase of a $1 million German-made washer for our commercial laundry business. Allow me the luxury of embellishment.

My boss at the time, the company CEO, thrived in an engineering background. He measured ROI on everything, almost. I'll explain that statement shortly.

Every piece of equipment, each new vehicle purchased, every square inch of building had to have an ROI associated with the cost thereof. Yes, everything must produce a bottom line. He did not, however, take this very sound and good sense practicality to the greatest of the company assets . . . at the time . . . me!

Embellishing further . . . Our company employed 90 percent of the local Baptist church's organization and on numerous occasions felt compelled to donate to the many causes explained to us by the minister of said congregation. The minister, quite gracious and appreciative, often promised to bring his good friend Muhammad Ali in to visit my boss and me sometime in the future. *Yeah, right,* I often mused.

Anyway, one day as I sat in the CEO's office (probably discussing the ROI on the million-dollar washer), the front gate security guard rang the president's office and informed us that the good minister *and* "the Greatest Fighter of All Times" were in the lobby.

Chills covered my body and blood rushed to my brain. Could

this be true? Would fate allow me to kneel before the Champ? Please keep in mind that I've never been what you'd call a student of the art of boxing, although I've had several fights myself. After each fight, however, I did not talk to Howard Cosell . . . I talked to the bail bondsman!

Well, within minutes the minister and my hero, Muhammad Ali, entered the CEO's office. *Awe* is not even close to describing my feelings at that particular moment.

After polite and gratifying kudos, the preacher asked about our business. I wanted to scream! Here we sit with the Greatest Boxer of All Times and the minister wished to hear about the laundry? Please, give me a break. It does get worse, however.

Our brilliant engineering CEO could not allow the opportunity of ROI description to elude the moment at hand and began his dissertation of the bottom line achievement of one million-dollar German washing machine. I was crazy at this point.

Fortunately, the Champ wasn't interested in German technology and decided it time to captivate the group with his magic show. I went into shock. Could it be I had entered the Twilight Zone? Was this surreal surrounding a dream of incomprehensible meaning? Nah, it was just as simple as my boss had a bottom line (ROI for German washers), the minister had a bottom line (needing donations), and Ali's bottom line was practicing his new vocation—the poet, fighter, magic man! My bottom line was much less complicated: get the Champ to sign a fifty-dollar bill. I believe I had to be the only one of the group that truly accomplished the bottom line in total that day.

Anyhow, I watched in respectful wonder as Ali made a red scarf disappear into his big rubber thumb and levitate by raising one foot while tiptoeing on the other foot. Needless to say, I have witnessed better magic shows, but what the heck. Who ain't going to cheer anything the Greatest Fighter Known to Man does?

Magic show completed, we toured the plant and the place went crazy. "ALI! ALI! ALI!" four hundred employees chanted in unison. It was a great day and Ali did sign my fifty-dollar bill in the parking lot: *"BEST WISHES, MUHAMMAD ALI."* For a moment, I forgot the German million-dollar washer.

This is indeed a true story, but what the heck does it have to do with "everybody has a bottom line"?

Here goes. . . .

Several days after the great Ali magic show, I entered the CEO's office in a somber mood, with a soulful expression upon my brow.

"Is everything OK, son?" my thoughtful boss inquired.

"Not really," I said, attempting to look like a boneless puppy.

"What's bothering you?" came the response of my concerned leader.

I replied, "Well, you know, I want you to quit treating me like a human being."

"Huh?" came back his reply, and I knew he was caught in my moment of reality-check time.

"I want to be treated like a German-made continuous-batch washing machine from now on," I joyfully proclaimed.

My boss always knew that I was at least half-crazy, and I'm sure it was moments like this that aided in the perception development of his young COO.

"What in the world are you talking about now?" he asked in a somewhat irritable tone.

I had him! I was ready! I fired the silver bullet! "Well, for the past six months, all I've heard about is the ROI for the new German washer and its impact on the bottom line. If you would begin to measure my performance by the exact same method, you would readily see that my ROI and bottom line contribution is much greater than your new laundry machine. Thus, by comparing me accordingly, my real net worth will be recognized and you will feel compelled to increase my compensation dramatically!"

Brilliant, absolutely staggering logic and comparative presentation, I thought to myself.

My introspecting boss gave my statement careful thought for all of thirty seconds and told me to get out of his office and go to work.

I did not get a raise and sulked the darkened laundry hallways feeling much like the Maytag man.

Lesson of the day?

C.B.P. ROI applies to everything in business and generally is associated with hard assets. But always remember that people are the greatest asset and everybody has a bottom line. *Find it, develop it, and reward it!*

The Bottom Lines

Owners, Stockholders, and Investors

- This group shares the same bottom line almost exclusively.
- Determine the necessary bottom line for the one putting up the money first.

    * The business must provide this bottom-line result before any other consideration, and that bottom line is rarely anything other than one of two things: long-term growth and value increase or send me the cash on a regular basis.

- This group must, however, be careful and not allow the deadly sin of greed to blind the long-term vision.

C.B.P. Inside Lesson: Owners', stockholders', and investors' greed is the reason for many businesses taking the toilet ride.

Key Employees

C.B.P. Any key employee that does not generate in new net cash double his compensation every year *is not a true key employee.*

Side Issue. I absolutely hate the hiring and pay structure of most government functions. Have you *ever* met, talked to, had to deal with a government employee? See any motivation? Experience any creativity? Feel like you're caught up in the movie *Night of the Living Dead*?

Why?

Real simple. Most are marking time waiting to go to Job Class 6 from Job Class 5. Not rewarded based on contribution, rather rewarded for showing up for a certain period of time and almost brain-dead functional participation in doda doda activity. *Monkey see . . . Monday do* syndrome.

C.B.P. Simple Lesson: Cost-of-living raises suck! Pay for achievement without a doesn't-make-sense cap.

Back to: *Key Employees.*

- Key employees are paid to achieve the goal, the budget, and the owner/investor requirements.
- Key employees should be additionally compensated for achievement *beyond* the agreed-to result as fairly as the owner/investors. Realizing, of course, that everything is relative. The risk takers eat the bigger part of the pie but at least give the overachieving key employee a decent-size piece. Crumbs from the plate can most often make key employees hungry and looking elsewhere.

C.B.P. Key employees make your bottom line happen. You *must find their bottom line and make it happen when* yours *has been realized.*

C.B.P. You can never overpay a key employee if investors are smiling.

The Little People

I have worked for two types of companies:

1. Those with owners who realized that the little people were the engine that drove the machine.
2. Those with owners who thought the little people were the mules that pulled the wagon.

Read 1 and 2 again, carefully. Although similar in interpretation, there is a major variance in the mental application for both the owners/managers and the employee.

Side Story: In the forty-seven different plants I've managed across these United States, I would venture to say that I knew almost all of the little people, many of whom I knew quite well.

Case in point: One of the last plants under my guidance was located in South Texas, very close to the Mexican border. We hired a very big man of Mexican origin who was covered with some very exotic and colorful tattoos. He had recently been released from jail for pot trafficking. He needed a second chance, and we gave it to him.

During my monthly three-day visits to this particular plant, it became my practice to frequent the only bar in town with my local management team. Needless to say, several of the little people enjoyed the same watering hole. I quickly levitated to the honesty of the big Mexican ex-convict that worked for us performing the nastiest job in the plant and for minimum wage. I grew to love this guy and often enjoyed several long-neck Buds with him.

Over the course of the next year, I learned about his wife and children, whom he loved a great deal. He told me about his tough upbringing and how he'd learned some very valuable lessons the hard way. This was indeed an honest man that only wished to take care of his family and do so with honor. And you know what? Most of the little people are much bigger than a lot of stupid "managers" even realize.

I watched my friend, my employee, and a darn good man receive three different promotions and double his hourly compensation that year. I think I was prouder of him than all of the other six hundred employees under my leadership.

Now along the way and during a weak moment, I employed a staff employee with "production expertise" as his claim to fame. During one of my monthly visits, I brought the expert with the New York attitude along. He pranced and strutted through the plant like the only rooster in Arkansas. As he approached the semi-secure area for new merchandise, he picked up a bundle of product and confronted my big Mexican employee and friend. The New Yorker, *don't I look important* expert inquired, "What's to stop me from picking this up and just walking out the back door?"

My big Mexican employee was quick to answer and to the point: "Well I guess, if you try, I will kick your ass!" Promotion number four was soon to follow.

My point in this story is simple.

C.B.P. Everybody *has a bottom line. The further down the organization you reach and realize, the stronger your company will become.*

Help, encourage, train, and get to know the little people. Take careful care of them and they will become a fine-tuned engine that will always outperform the mules.

Customer Base

Do you know the bottom line of your customers? It's always one of four things:

1. Price
2. Quality

3. Service
4. Personal relationship,

number 4 being of greatest value and number 1 of least value.

I hate 800 numbers going to impersonal phone bank operators: "What's your problem, Mr. Jones? Someone will get back to you." *Never* works nearly as well as, "Hey, Charlie, what can I do for you?"

C.B.P. Your competitors will steal all your "Mr. Jones" customers and you will continue to sell to the "Hey, Charlies"!

Build a business retention system that focuses on the *solutions* to a customer's concern, *within twenty-four hours,* and be a *friendly* member of the management team. All any of us ever want is a quick and familiar resolution.

C.B.P. A company that responds to each customer as if he were the only customer, will almost always keep that customer.

One final point: VOICE MAIL SUCKS!

C.B.P. When you get so big and important that a customer's call can wait, prepare to add additional salespeople.

Everybody Has a Bottom Line!

- If you are to succeed, enhance this principle with great consideration, forethought and sincerity.
- <u>What's the bottom line for the owner, stockholder, investor?</u>

  * Without clear knowledge and achievement of this, <u>no one</u> will ever be satisfied.

- <u>Establish the bottom line for all key employees.</u>

  * You might own the train, but the engineer gets it

from point A to point B. His bottom-line attainment will always get you to yours.

- <u>Search for and find the bottom line for the little people.</u>
    * The ignorance of this principle creates laziness, absenteeism, thieves, and workers' comp lawyers.
    * Take care of the engine and watch your train run smoothly and fast.

12
Basic Organizational Skills

I have no doubt that more business books are written attempting to address organizational skills than diet books are written for fat people. Now that I think about it, both have a lot in common . . . let's get lean!

The best organizational/basic planning book I ever read was *The One Minute Manager*. The book was written by a Ph.D. and M.D. Seems a bit odd, as I've often wondered how men so smart and educated ever found a truth so simple and applicable.

But like the diet books or *The One Minute Manager*, organizational skills must be simple and repetitive. They must rule the day not be assembled as the day progresses.

Organization Skill Stories

I once employed a general manager of high integrity, with a strong work ethic, and totally void of any organizing ability. He was the classic example of the in-basket manager.

In-Basket Manager Explained

A manager that has at minimum six stacks of stuff on his desk waiting and competing for the most dust collection. One pile is always important, one pile is never important, and the other four fall somewhere in between. However, none of the piles ever reached priority status because none will ever be addressed. Mr. In-Basket, sadly, like many managers, has a different approach to managing his business.

Do you know this person? He sits nervously, fidgets frequently, drinks a lot of coffee, gets tired thinking about the six piles on his desk and waiting for something to do, anything to do! That describes my in-basket general manager perfectly.

Whatever was placed in front of him became the immediate priority. Relative importance, ROI contribution, delegation possibilities, were void in his thinking process. Often I would remark how his desk looked like the final destination for BFI. Even humiliation didn't affect the in-basket manager.

C.B.P. Busy and productive don't always walk down the same street hand in hand.

During one of my weekly visits to the IB's plant, I informed him that I would like to review his P&L after I met with our corporate engineer, currently building a major addition to the existing facility.

Thirty minutes later, I went searching for the IB general manager. He had disappeared. As I continued my search, the receptionist informed me that my missing general manager had left the plant to purchase gas for the forklift. Needless to say, I was not very happy at that point. I mean really, this guy employed ninety-five people, the president of the company (me) was in town to discuss really important stuff, and he's the only one available to go buy five gallons of gasoline?

But fortunately, instead of becoming angry, I decided Mr. In-Basket was about to learn how to become Mr. Out-Basket. When he returned from his most recent in-basket activity, smelling of 87 Octane, I sat behind his desk with a fifty-five-gallon empty barrel. The times they were a-changin'!

I told the receptionist to hold all calls (unless a customer) and hung a handmade sign: DO NOT DISTURB, on the IB's door. We began pile reclamation:

> Pile One: Books and industry-related articles he planned to read dating back twelve months. Into the barrel in total. I advised him to stop planning to read stuff he would never read.
>
> Pile Two: New sales contracts and associated support documents. I permanently delegated the future review of said documents to the sales manager.
>
> Piles Three and Four: Mostly stuff he saved to do that time relegated no longer too important or someone else took the initiative to already do it. Into the barrel it all went.
>
> Pile Five: Memos from me left unanswered. Of course, we saved the entire lot.
>
> Pile Six: Things he should have done, been doing, or would have to do. Saved it!

For the first time in his long career, he could see his desk. I stopped him from fetching a two-wheel dolly and hauling the half-full barrel to the dumpster. I suggested that we call the janitor so I might not have to wait for fifteen minutes while he took the dumpster trip, although the fresh air might have helped eliminate the lingering smell of forklift fuel.

The Movie Star Manager

During the same period of time when I was managing Mr. In-Basket, I also controlled a large facility in a New Jersey ghetto. The location housed my regional vice president for the Northeast, a handsome Italian chap, well groomed, and immaculately attired. I did however, being a country boy, have a real problem with his polished fingernails. For him, that was Yankee sophistication. For me, it was hard to imagine sitting in a nail salon and discussing whatever ladies discuss at such intimate moments.

Now this gentlemen did not have the in-basket disease . . . he acquired the *no basket* virus! Our company had recently built new offices in the ghetto plant, and my regional vice president was permitted to replace his office furniture. As you can imagine, a fashionable New York Italian executive would only buy the best (especially when it's somebody else's money).

I first entered his new office and became instantly impressed with the beautiful cherry office furniture, *and* lots of it. On one wall rested a picture of some great Civil War battle, and the opposite wall was covered with past meaningless and not that great achievement awards. The ego man with polished nails glowed in his new environment. It does get better.

On his desk and conference table tops lay beveled cut *mirrored* glass. No pencils, calculator, notepad, or six piles of dumpster stuff . . . I'm telling you, nothing! I asked my movie star regional vice president if he ever tired of seeing himself in his desktop mirror. He remarked that he rarely ever noticed. Yeah, right.

Last Example—The Filer

Some eleven years ago, I had the great and lasting good fortune of meeting Pam Kelly. Pam and I met in the same industry, and she has worked under my direction for the duration of our time together. Pam is highly intelligent, committed, talented, and beautiful. She is now also my wife, which is great evidence to my intellectual capacity.

Pam Kelly has, over the course of the past eleven years, held several positions of importance, the last being executive vice president of the British public company I managed as president.

Without her help and motivation I would never have accomplished as much or written this book. I love and respect her immensely.

That aside, she did, however, have one small fault when it came to organizational skills. Pam Kelly Bryant was a filer. No matter how important or insignificant, Pam would establish a file for it. Her files were at least ten times the volume of my own, and God forbid that she discard anything. She was well organized, but it could take days to find a really important something in among the national archives of her office. (This has been written with Pam's permission, as she is my boss after the five o'clock whistle blows!)

Getting to the point, basic organizational skills are not only important; long-term success depends on your ability to organize properly and daily.

C.B.P. *A minute wasted could be a dollar lost.*

Basic Organizational Skills

1. *In-Basket:* Once a day you should review *everything* that needs to be looked at, *by you.* Preferably in the evening.

    a. Junk junk mail without a second's review.
    b. If it can be addressed *quickly,* do it now and attempt to pass on. Pass on stuff by utilizing *brief* stickem' messages.
    c. If documented follow-up is required, write short, to-the-point, anticipated-reaction-time memos.
    d. At the end of the day, your in-basket should be empty.

2. *Out Basket:* There are two:

    a. Trash can
    b. Keep it moving

 * All the important transferable stuff reviewed and addressed from your in-basket review.

3. *Filing*

    a. Do your own, and you'll always know where to find it.

4. *Tomorrow's Stack*

    a. After review of all in-basket materials, the following path is:

 * Trash can
 * Been addressed and resides in out-basket
 * Needs more thought and reaction to, goes *in priority order* in your tomorrow-things-to-do stack.

5. *Legal Pad Today Activity Listing*

    a. Utilize a basic yellow legal pad (unless you're the movie star type with polished nails—then get the pink ones!).
    b. In *priority order* list everything you need to do, including the in-basket carryover that remains in your tomorrow's desk stack.
    c. List activities for the next three days on the legal pad.
    d. Add a bottom and final heading of "Other," for everything that needs addressing but is not im-

portant enough to do in the three-day priority activity schedule.

Always keep in mind that most days you probably won't get through every item on that day's priority list. That's OK; just transfer the item to the next day's list.

After the evening in-basket review and disposals, you should complete your legal pad activity listing. Make this a priority. Plan for tomorrow today! When you start anew the next morning, your mind is fresh and your plan is set.

    6. *Meetings with Key People*
    Just because you're the boss doesn't give you the right to interrupt a subordinate's daily plan, and more important, you should not allow the reverse to happen because you are the boss!

The previously noted five basic organization tools apply to the entire management team.

    a. Establish a weekly file for each manager reporting directly to you.
* Place anything that needs review from your in-basket review *or* that might come up during the day in the direct report employee file.
    b. Schedule an exact meeting time and stay with it. In most cases I find daily, in the morning, fifteen to thirty minutes, works best. Now you know and your key employees know what needs to be done and everyone can get to it without constant and unnecessary interruption throughout the day.

I am not saying that times won't come and things arise that

need immediate attention and discussion. But I am telling you that they are the exception, not the rule.

7. *Start Each New Year*

   a. Every year I would start January by first clearing every piece of paper from every file and properly storing those files for twelve months.
   b. At the same time I discarded all files that were now one year old.
   c. All my new files were empty at the beginning of the year and it was absolutely amazing how *rarely* I ever had to go to the previous year's files. Obviously, this doesn't apply to government regulations or CYA material if you work for someone else.

C.B.P. If you are not consistently well organized, your business will become disorganized and your employees will become mirror watchers . . . and it will be your mirror they are looking into.

13

Building Wealth and for Whom

- Why are you in business?
- Why do you wish to expand your business?
- Why do you wish to start a business?

If you've purchased my book and made it this far, I will assume you fit in one of the above categories.

In my opinion, and that of, I suppose, anyone else that is about to or is currently in his own business, the answer is: IT'S ABOUT BUILDING WEALTH.

I can hear you all now: "Well, thank you very much, Mr. Bryant for that extremely insightful proclamation . . . DUH?! Like we didn't already clearly understand, Mr. Bryant, why we keep busting our humps. It's about building wealth, stupid!"

OK then, I'll give you that. However, I'd be willing to bet that a lot of small-business people, and I've met some of you, understand that basic premise but never evaluate and address the long-term, ultimate goal. You just get too busy to realize, *I'm building long-term wealth.*

Let's examine:

The British company I last worked for happened to be the largest dry cleaner in England and the United States. Several years ago, an attempt was made to sell dry-cleaning franchises across the country. The concept was good and the results a disaster. Businesspeople such as you and I dreamed of becoming entrepreneurs.

They longed for building a family business and searched for the building wealth opportunity. But you know for every "I brought a McDonald's franchise for ten thousand dollars" there are a thousand "I bought a dry cleaner or a printing franchise and lost my butt in the process."

Let's just take a moment and review a "hypothetical dry cleaner" franchise.

Cost to purchase franchise	$250,000
Cost for equipment	150,000
Cost for I now own a drycleaner	$400,000
Projected weekly sales	8,000
Projected weekly profit (cash flow)	12%
	$960 ROI

If you financed 50 percent of the initial business, you will, in say, approximately ten years, pay off the debt and recover your original investment.

On the other side of the equation is:

I ain't that stupid.
I have a normal job making $50,000 per year.
I invested my original $200,000 in mutual funds.
In ten to twelve years, I can probably retire.

So why would anyone buy a dry-cleaning franchise? I attribute it to the M&M theory . . . Moron with Money.

A true-life example occurred while I lived in Cincinnati. I did not know the guy, but a neighbor of mine did and recalled the story.

The individual was offered and accepted early retirement with a big buyout from Proctor and Gamble. He then purchased a well-known dry-cleaning franchise. So far so good. What he failed to realize, however, was that the success of any drycleaner depends on: LOCATION, LOCATION, LOCATION. This guy's dry-cleaning shop had to be at the worst location of any dry cleaner in America. The store sat at the back of a strip shopping center with a real estate office and a Rent-A-Tool business directly in front of his operation. The only way you'd ever know he existed was if you stopped and ate at the local chili dog establishment at the end of the shopping center.

To make matters worse, he purchased the dry-cleaning franchise just as the biggest downturn in dry-cleaning history began.

So what's my point? Neither the people that purchased our dry-cleaning franchises nor the guy with the early retirement bucks bought an opportunity for "building wealth." They both purchased themselves a job, and not a very good one at that.

Now let's review some basic facts for consideration.

1. You are thinking about starting your own business. Why?
   a. Building long-term sustainable wealth for yourself.
   b. Building it and selling it at a great return.
   c. Building it for your children.

In any case, a, b, or c, the following applies:

1. What's my cash in . . . plus?
2. How much time will I have to give and what's the value of my time . . . plus?
3. What's the risk?
4. What's the ROI/cash out?

Oversimplification, of course, but how many small businesses fail each year because someone did not ask such simple questions? I'd venture to say quite a lot.

Spend the necessary time and money to properly research a

potential wealth-building opportunity on the front end before you jump into a situation and find out all you did was buy yourself a job, and one you can't quit!

   2. Let's say you currently own a business. The first thing I'd do is find out accurately how much it would be worth if you sold it today.

Back to the dry-cleaning example. For years, the going rate for purchasing a dry-cleaning company has been fifty times weekly sales. *Today* that has dropped to twenty-five times *if* you can find a buyer. I'd venture to say there are a lot of old dry cleaners out there that continue to believe that fifty to one still applies. Their building-wealth opportunity is, unfortunately, a smoke screen.

Let's simplify:

- The market value of your business currently is a net $250,000 if sold immediately.
- You know that the future of your business and the long-term growth expectations are equal to or greater than the GNP.
- The cost to add new business is 50 percent or less than the ultimate value added, if you sell it in the future.
- Historical market value appraisals have remained stable or experienced an increase.
- You are having fun.
- Your children enjoy the business.

If the answers to these statements are to the positive, stay with it. If the answers are negative, sell the business, invest the gain, and find a good job for the next few years.

Simple Truths

1. If the business you start takes up-front investment, involves risk, and the end result is all you have is a pretty good job, *Don't Do It!*
2. If the business continues to or has defined growth opportunities on the cash out side, *Do It!*
3. If you believe the business is at market value peak and risk versus reward is a frequent consideration, *Sell It!*
4. If you're building the business for the next generation, remember: *"The first generation starts the business. The second generation builds the business. The third generation screws it up!"* So, if you're building the business for your children, you would probably be better off sending them to law school to specialize in environmental or workers' compensation litigation. Or, for your grandchildren, establish a trust fund that can't be touched until they're fifty and buy them an advanced Nintendo!

Now you, my friend, should enjoy the wealth that you have worked so hard to build. And if you haven't quite built that wealth yet, just be glad you bought this book so you can get started.

14
When to Buy a Business

The decision of when to buy *or* when to sell *will* always be extremely difficult. Blood, sweat, and tears are all three necessary ingredients in the preparation of such important decisions. The future of your business can be greatly enhanced *or* destroyed by too quick and uncareful review of such a determination.

When-To-Buy Opportunities

1. To enter into a new business or expand into a new market.
2. To expand existing market share.
3. To take advantage of a fire sale.

1. Entering into a New Business or Expanding into a New Market

- Make no mistake: this carries the highest risk of the three when-to-buy opportunities. Failure to analyze every aspect of the potential purchase will someday make you wish you were not so eager.
- It's all risk and reward. However, being the conservative

type, I look at the risk with much greater perplexity than I approach the reward side.

Questions to Ask and Answer prior to Buying a New Business or Market

- Will the <u>basic</u> cash payback be accomplished in five years or less?
- Can I resell the business in five years for what I originally paid for it *and* recoup any additional capital put into the business during those five years?

If the answer to the above is "no" or "I'm not sure," remember:

C.B.P. You can't swim in quicksand.

Major Points of Reality

- In priority order, less risk being first: CDs, stock market, blackjack, buying a business, slot machines.
- It's rare that anyone ever makes the decision to sell his business because he is making tons of money.
- Never trust someone else's financials.
- Never believe the seller.
- Always talk to the customers of the seller.
- Only hire a consultant in the business appraisal review *if* said consultant *thoroughly understands* the business.
- Outsource paid accounting firms generally generate know-it-all math teachers with a great ability to analyze balance sheets. Don't need them.
- In *most cases* the value of a business is not clearly indicated on the balance sheet. The balance sheet details hard assets, easily defined, found, and real value determined.

- The *real worth* of a business is most often realized in the "soft assets", i.e.,

  * Management team
  * Employee longevity
  * Customer retention
  * Pricing
  * Competitive environment
  * Growth potential and ratio to GNP
  * Success of competition
  * Last three years' growth at the top and bottom line

2. Expanding Existing Market

- Much safer than buying a new business for no other reason than you already have an existing profitable growing base. If you don't, then please skip to the next chapter, *"When to Sell"*
- Variable accounting in this particular decision mode is either half-stupid or half-smart. Since I have utilized the practice often, it must be half-smart. Every business has fixed overhead. Adding quick top-line dollars to the existing base should *always* add more profit per revenue dollar than each previous dollar generated prior to acquisition; i.e., I have a business that generates $20,000 per week at a 20 percent profit (cash) rate. Net weekly cash = 4,000 or 20%. I purchase a small competitor that does $10,000 per week doing the same things I do with similar cost and pricing. I can add the business without expanding my facility, adding to the G&A, and I do so without the associated cost of a new sales effort that would have been necessary if I had secured the 10,000 per week by utilizing my existing sales team.

Every business is different, but I believe a good rule of thumb, *if you've done your homework,* is that adding revenue via acquisition to your existing base will increase profit on the additional volume, double that of your existing profit.

Existing business revenue = $20,000 = $4,000 20%
Acquisition   = $10,000 = $4,000 40%
Net results   = $30,000 = $8,000 27% Profit

Now, what should I pay for this business?

Obviously, the five-year simple cash payback rule still applies, but you can pay a higher multiple for purchasing add-on business than buying a *new business* because of fixed cost coverage. I.e., I buy a new business at $10,000 per week in revenue delivering 20 percent profit (cash). This business has facility and G&A overhead cost. I know that the business generates $2,000 per week profit (because of my careful and thorough review). I can therefore afford to pay $520,000 and meet my five-year payback goal.

Note: If inventories and equipment are old, the cost of upgrading, fixing, or replacing certainly fits into the five-year payback scenario.

On the other hand, I purchase a $10,000 per week business and simply add that volume to my existing business with no increase to fixed cost. *Now* that business will generate $4,000 per week in cash. Does this mean you should pay $1,040,000 for the business? *No!* It means you can up the offer and afford to be more competitive without nearly the risk associated with purchasing that same business as a new stand-alone operation.

So What Are the Rules of Engagement for Expanding Existing Market by Buying Additional Revenues?

- The five-year payback rule still applies, but the amount paid can be greater than buying a new, stand-alone business simply because of the fixed overhead coverage that exists.
- You obviously eliminate a competitor.
- Carefully review the synergies. There are usually many.
- Attempt to always hold back a portion of the purchase price for a period long enough to determine you did not catch a left hook.
- Seller financing is a precious thing.
- It helps if the customer base is a contractual base.

3. Taking Advantage of a Fire Sale

C.B.P. Usually when the smoke clears, you'll find someone got burnt.

C.B.P. When it appears to be too good to be true . . . it most often is.

Fire sale opportunities usually exist because the seller is stupid or the seller is stupid! I'll explain. Too stupid to know the real worth of his business or too stupid to manage it, so now you can buy the owner's mistakes. Ninety-nine percent of the time, I think you'll find too stupid to manage is the case.

So, should I look at a fire sale? Only if . . .

- You can purchase the business for <u>less</u> than it costs you to add new revenues via your own operational sales effort.
- Pay no more then 80 percent for the customer base. . . . You will probably lose 20 percent in the near term.
- You really *need* quick top-line revenues for an *important* reason, i.e., in the next year, you're going to sell your busi-

ness and the additional revenue will increase the value more than the cost to purchase it.

Now that I have shared my twenty-five years of experience in buying businesses, allow me to proclaim some real-life, lived-through, unbelievable stupidity.

Example One

In the late eighties, I worked for a company that was financed almost completely by *junk bonds*. I did not realize at the time just how appropriate the name for this type of financing actually was . . . pure, unadulterated *junk!*

When the smoke cleared . . . a bunch of investors got burnt!

If it's too good to be true . . . it was!

Try this one on and see how it fits.

This company grew from zero to a hundred million dollars in annual revenue in a few short years. The rapid growth came via acquisition via junk bond financing.

The industry we were in as a whole generated 10 to 12 percent profit. The unsecured interest on debt was 14 percent. As well, we had secured debt. Combined, the total debt burden for this company equaled 19 percent of total revenue! Now that's beyond stupid. But you know what? The biggest bond holder (25 percent) was a major insurance company. You'd think before investing *millions* of dollars a big insurance company would have a junior accountant at least look at the industry they were about to invest in.

Junior accountants for major insurance company calculation: Business generates 12 percent cash. Debt load = 19 percent = ain't gonna work = triple-stupid!

Example Two

For many years I have been heavily involved in acquisitions, to the tune of about $80 million spent. Did I ever screw up? You bet I did. But when I did, it was with somebody else's money, so learn that lesson carefully if all you got is *your money!*

Another company I worked for allowed me to purchase a small acquisition in Nashville, Tennessee, generating $17,000 per week in top-line revenue.

We determined that break-even would come at $23,000 and 12 percent profit at $30,000.

Lo and behold, it came to my attention that a small independent was considering the possibility of selling his business, $11,000 per week. Just what the doctor ordered.

I *eagerly* meet the fella and bonded immediately. A good-old-boy type that liked to fish and slug down a twelve-pack of Old Milwaukee from the back of his pickup truck. His down-home, Barney Fife charm easily translated into trust for me, or so I thought.

I should have remembered a lesson I learned in Nam about the Viet Cong: "They smile at you in the daytime and plant land mines in the road at night!"

I guess this old country boy was a VC too . . . *Very Clever.*

Anyway, all the rules I presented in this chapter I threw out the window. After all, I was the guru of acquisitions. I could judge character with the best of them. I was smarter than this old country boy any day of the week.

Long story short, I paid a premium price, cash, all up front, after hardly any <u>real</u> review of the financials, which he said didn't exist.

The end result was his $11,000 per week business turned out to be $8,000 and the entire deal made me look like a complete fool . . . and rightfully so.

Basic truism based on the previous two examples:
C.B.P. It's easier to spot a wolf in sheep's clothing than to recognize a beagle dressed like a rabbit.

15
When to Sell a Business

Entrepreneurs, it seems, have a much harder time with the final decision to sell than managers of public companies, and rightfully so. After all, you gave birth to the business. You raised it and nurtured it through the growing pain years. It became your spouse, your family, your reason for living, and now the unspeakable consumes your every thought. I must deliver my creation into the hands of the enemy . . . poor baby.

Forget all that emotional stuff; there is really only one solitary reason we all show up each day. I don't care if you are the janitor or you are the owner. We are all there for . . . THE MONEY!!!

Oh, I can hear some of you now. Mad as hell and thinking that I'm the cold-hearted type that never measured the intangibles.

OK, I'll give you that. Let's review several fundamental intangibles:

1. I care about the people that have dedicated their lives to my business! "Very good, Mr. Owner. So give them all stock, large raises, and show us where your big intangible heart is."
2. I don't know what I'd do without my company. "Golf, sailboat, travel, read, go back to school, climb mountains, race cars, enjoy the kids, watch birds, hunt arrowheads, raise a garden, play the stock market . . .

Understand, most likely fifty to eighty percent of your life is over. Enjoy what's left."
3. I'm building the business for my kids! "Nine out of ten times you'll be sorry, not appreciated, and unwelcomed in the business you built. Why have to endure such agony? Sell the business and give the kids some cash; they probably don't deserve or understand the business anyway and most likely will screw it up."

Now that I have soundly defeated your intangible emotional thinking process, we are back to why sell your business . . . FOR THE MONEY!!

C.B.P. Absolute Rule: "If you sell your business and get enough for it to do everything else in life you wish to do, it is a no-brainer.

When Should I Sell My Business?

- When you are tired and it's no longer fun.
- When you have lost the competitive advantage and market share is diminishing.
- When long-term investment requirements might reach out more years than you have left to live.
- When the offer is larger than the true market value.
- When you decide there are other things more important in life.
- When you're working harder at the end than in the beginning.

What Is My Business Worth?

Who knows? Now how's that for advice from a small-business consultant? But in all seriousness, determining the value of your business is based on that criterion associated with the particular business you're in and available buyers. But the same rule should apply to selling your business as is applicable in buying a business, the five-year payback rule: i.e., take your existing P&L statement and start with the last year's bottom line:

- Last year bottom line
- plus
- All depreciated P&L line item amounts
- plus
- All your compensation and other funny money, IRS-hidden, I got away with,

personal funding = Net generated cash
                              x five years
net business worth =

Please understand the five-year payback method has been applicable to my particular industry and yours might be higher or, for that matter, lower, in any case, whatever the market will bear, and you should carefully study market valuation before any consideration is given to selling out.

Should I Sell the Business Myself?

- Almost always, never! You will be emotionally attached and, generally speaking, believe your business is worth more than it is.
- Never trust the buyer.
- Cash is better than stock *most* of the time.
- Get it all up front.
- *Sell* the A/Rs.

- Never stay with the purchasing company longer than a short transitional period.

C.B.P. The Fourth Biggest Lie: We are buying your business, and nothing is going to change.

Best Selling-Out Story—Undersold

Twice this has happened to me and twice the parent company was a publicly traded British company. In both instances, the parent companies' big brains knew very little about their U.S. investment. But both felt a strong need to keep the potential sale secret from the U.S. management team.

As COO of one and CEO of the other, I begged and pleaded with the parent company to allow me to arrange the sale by competitively shopping the business. In both cases, I was denied. Only one secretive bidder would be allowed. First company sold at 65 percent of market value. Second company sold at 85 percent of market value. *MILLIONS* left on the table.

If you decide to sell your business, *tell your key people.* Tell them why and reward them financially for aiding you and seeing the sale through to completion.

C.B.P. I've Got a Secret *was an old television show, not a legitimate approach for selling your business.*

Hit the Jackpot

In this book you will readily notice that I have been careful not to mention the names of any person. This will be the one exception.

At the tender age of thirty I met Quentin Wahl. At the time, I held a small portion of ownership in a family business located in

Mobile, Alabama. Quentin lived and operated a similar business in Toronto. We were approximately the same age and developed a lasting friendship that began because Quentin wished to know my thoughts on the business we were both attempting to manage and grow.

I will tell you that Quentin Wahl was creative, innovative, and not afraid to take a *calculated* risk. He built one of the best-known and most successful businesses in North America in our associated industry. And you know what else? He had a heck of a lot of fun and his team loved working for him.

Now here is a highly successful businessman, the company is growing rapidly, his profit numbers are remarkable, and he's having fun, and yet he sold the company. "Why?" do you ask. FOR THE MONEY! Since the sale of his business, Quentin has climbed some of the world's biggest mountains, raced cars, bought homes all over the world, and enjoyed raising his children and sharing each day with his bride. He achieved a remarkable lifestyle, *because* he worked hard, intelligently, and stayed the course. But most important, Quentin knew *when* to sell his business.

C.B.P. Timing is everything, or so they say. But right timing with no money is boredom the hard way.

16
Adapt; Improvise; Overcome

You've no doubt realized by now that I have a propensity and take great pride in recalling my experiences as a member of the United States Marine Corps. You may have also seen the great, should-have-won-an-Academy-Award movie *Heartbreak Ridge,* starring the greatest of all macho men, Clint Eastwood. He portrayed a Marine Corps drill instructor, bad to the bone, and meaner than *three* junkyard dogs.

I'll never forget the scene in the movie when he laid down the most basic of Marine Corps principles: marines succeed with fewer people, old equipment, odds stacked against them, because marines are forced to learn how to: ADAPT . . . IMPROVISE . . . OVERCOME. . . . I proudly admit that a great deal of my success is due to my experiences in the Marine Corps. You see, when I arrived at Parris Island with my long blond hair blowing in the wind, I learned real quickly how to *adapt* . . . without any hair.

As I spent many a lonely night on some hill named after a number, or walking through rice paddies waiting to hear the heart-warming shout of, *"INCOMING!"* I learned to *improvise.* And when I witnessed death and questioned my very own sanity and the truthful reason why we were fighting this senseless war, I was forced to *overcome.*

Business, I believe, is very much like the Marine Corps. It's tough, never-ending, demanding, and there are no excuses for failure. As well, business can be similar to my experiences in Vietnam. Why am I here? What am I doing? Is there no end in sight? Will I survive? How do we win this war?

Almost all business books are written as how-tos. I guess this book is not much different, with the exception of my down-home humor, exhorted experiences, and been there, done that clarity.

But there is more to business than P&L statements, balance sheets, stockholders' equity, right way, wrong way analysis. There's something *deeper.* That thing that occasionally twists inside your gut and causes a rapid increase to your heart rate. That thing is called Survival Reality! Some of us never experience it, and those that don't usually fail. Business KIAs.

This chapter is dedicated to that "Survival Reality." So that when your education fails, business plan dissolves, and people let you down, you can dig deeper, forgetting all the how-to books and previous lessons learned. If you fight in a war for a while or survive in business long enough, the time will come when you must face the deciding battle. It will come as a sniper round, silent and deadly. Like a trip wire that gives you instant notification . . . you are history! As the whistling sound in a dark night before the rocket lands besides you. It will come. And when it does, you must believe and be prepared to throw all caution to the wind. Business survival may depend on your ability to *adapt, improvise, and overcome.*

Adapt (verb): Adjust to be suitable for a new use or condition.

I have watched *and* participated in the failure of addressing critical moments in business decision adjustments because of the hesitancy to adapt more times than I care to elaborate on.

C.B.P. For entrepreneurs, the ability *for adaptation practice is too often a lesson learned after the fact.*

Why?

- I'm smarter than anyone else, so I must be right.
- I'll *force* the plan to work.
- I'll *force* the employee to *adapt.*

- I don't know how.

When?

- My ideas aren't working.
- The plan has failed.
- The employee has drawn a line in the sand.
- When I first knew that I don't know how to.

Best Adaptation Story

In 1979, I worked for a terrific family that owned the largest dry-cleaning company in our market area and a growing regional uniform rental business. One business was faced with a serious economic downturn, and the other had peaked. While both continued to do well, the handwriting appeared on the wall . . . these business opportunities will not get better.

Did we wish, hope and pray? No.

Did we wring our hands and cry about it? No.

Did we ignore the problem (like most managers) and disguise the inevitable with our own self-indulging ego . . . we're too good to fail attitudes? No.

We looked around ourselves for opportunity. In doing so, we began to question why, over the course of the past year, our company had found it necessary to employ three different janitorial companies to clean our corporate office. Each janitorial service had failed miserably. As we studied the janitorial business, we found they struggled with two basic but major problems:

1. Finding part-time workers at minimum wage.
2. Quality-focused systems.

Our existing business was labor-intensive, with low pay and

unskilled laundry workers. But our base of employees was dedicated, honest, hardworking, and they'd love to have part-time evening jobs. We were professional dry cleaners and a commercial uniform rental company with highly developed quality systems. In fact, we found the answers to the biggest problems faced by the janitorial business in a totally unrelated business, because we expanded our vision.

Armed with this knowledge, we purchased a small one-man janitorial business. We then developed and applied our existing business systems to this endeavor. As well, many of our loyal employees were eager to work several hours in the evening for our new janitorial expansion.

Within one year, the janitorial diversification exceeded $1 million in sales, or a 14 percent increase to our existing business base. *WE ADAPTED!*

Improvise (verb): make, invent, or arrange offhand.

C.B.P. Improvisation is a God-given talent like music or painting. It's not a college course, but it can be learned, if practiced.

Best Improvisation Story

Same company as adaptation story and approximately the same time period, dealing with the same problem. We now had three businesses, dry cleaning, uniform rental, and janitorial services.

In the dry-cleaning business, you spend a great deal of money and time advertising. Our company advertised in the newspaper, on television, and on the radio. We utilized an ad company from Milwaukee and spent big bucks doing so.

One day as we continued to focus on "adaptation opportunity," the realization came brightly forth that advertising was not just placing ads or buying radio spots; it was *ideas!* And you know what? Most of the time it was *our idea* that worked, not the ad agency's.

Within a matter of months, we were in a new business.... We started our own advertising agency from scratch. First year sales exceeded $500,000.

Overcome (verb): defeat

The Steve Bryant definition:

C.B.P. *The ability to* adapt *and* improvise *will always allow you to* overcome *the obstacle.*

Let's Review

- Because of our ability and willingness to *adapt,* we were driven to *improvise.* By adapting and improvising, we were able to *overcome* the challenge.
- There are always other opportunities that have a direct or sometimes indirect tie to the existing business you're in. Diversification? Maybe. Or maybe it's as simple as full utilization of assets, people, opportunities, and *ideas!*

C.B.P. *There is always more than one tree in any forest.*

- You can and should utilize your existing customer base for expansion opportunities. Think out of the box! In this case, many of our uniform rental customers became janitorial and advertising clients.
- This small $8 million company changed its strategy and motto to: "We are a marketing company that just happens to also be in the laundry business." In one short year, our existing base business grew by 21 percent, because we adapted, improvised and overcame.
- Our existing businesses were capital-intensive. The two

new diversifications *were not,* thus creating a much-improved cash flow environment for the total company.

Are you a company of pronouns and adjectives? Remember that all three words we've discussed in this chapter are verbs! Verbs mean action, and without a verb you don't have a proper sentence. As well, without constant action your business will slow and eventually stop.

C.B.P. Without the ability to adapt, improvise, *and* overcome, *you will never have the opportunity to maximize the opportunity.*

17
The Moral Thing

This obviously is not a religious manuscript, nor would I attempt in this writing to convert or convict anyone. I am a God-fearing man who studies his Bible daily and believes that prayer is as applicable to business as any classroom lesson taught at Harvard. Probably a *great deal* more applicable. After all, God did an absolutely magnificent job creating the universe. He just, unfortunately, seems to have a problem finding the right people for the job at hand.

Your particular devotion is of no consequence to me as it relates to this topic. However, I do believe that *all* religious fundamentals begin with and end with the same universal basic truth: "Do unto others as you'd wish them to do unto you."

I was forced once to read the publication *Mean Business* and prepare a report on how I would apply the lessons taught in that book to my group of businesses at the time. I found the book *Mean Business* to fall somewhere in-between *The Fall of the Roman Empire* and *Helter Skelter*. My report was written with a great deal of thought and consisted of one sentence: "Instead of focusing on *Mean Business,* why don't we first apply the principles of Good Business?" You know, my boss never responded to my report. It probably confused him with the complexity of honest simplification.

C.B.P. Fear for one's job will never develop love for the owner's goals.

So what do I mean when I say "the moral thing"?
I'll give you a good and easy comparison to gnaw on. Check the things you enjoy most from both lists:

The Moral Thing

_____ I enjoy being appreciated.
_____ I want my boss to like me.
_____ It's great to help a coworker.
_____ Boy, this company really pays me well.
_____ I can go talk to my boss when I have a problem.
_____ The company explained the reasons why.
_____ If I do better, the company does better.
_____ Setting goals is great.
_____ Achieving goals is even better.
_____ Being rewarded for achieving goals is morally right.
_____ I've never been lied to.
_____ There is no hidden agenda.
_____ I can't wait to get to work.
_____ I'm excited about sharing my new idea.
_____ I am needed.
_____ I am wanted.
_____ I am respected.

The Mean Business Thing

_____ Who gives a damn?
_____ My boss is an AK know-it-all.
_____ I like working with a bunch of spies and rats.
_____ I enjoy being paid like a migrant worker.
_____ I like to rat on my coworkers.
_____ Not knowing what's going on really motivates me.
_____ I'm glad the boss gets richer and I'm getting poorer.
_____ My first goal is not to get fired.

_____ My second goal is to not get caught doing nothing.
_____ My third goal is to file a bogus Worker's Comp claim.
_____ I like being a better liar than my boss.
_____ I can't wait until I'm laid off and draw unemployment!
_____ I like to call in sick once a week.
_____ All my ideas are stupid.
_____ Nobody needs a dummy like me.
_____ I hope nobody ever wants me to be more than the worthless, hopeless, self-centered, don't-give-a-damn person that this company has worked so hard to develop.

Get my point? Did I overdo the comparison? I don't know. It's you that has to check the checklist, and since only you will know, do it honestly. Are you the moral businessperson or the mean businessperson?

C.B.P. "Mean Business" practices have never in the history of the world started as the beginning of the process. They are always 100 percent of the time, at the end of all activity.

And who gets hurt? The little people, the ones who gave it their best. And who caused the failure? You did. I did. The owners, CEOs, and board of directors screwed it up. Then what happens? Why, the owner, CEO, or new hired gun calls it somebody else's fault and receives a bonus to shoot a bunch of innocent employees. They will explain it as:

- Turnaround situation;
- Fourth-quarter adjustment;
- Strategic plan; or, the worst of all,
- The austerity program.

C.B.P. Austerity programs are easily defined as the people at the top screwed up. Austerity programs today, prosperity tomorrow, bought out eventually.

Am I opposed to austerity programs or lean-and-mean conceptual thinking? Not at all, *if* you begin there. What I am opposed to is stupid leadership that created the need for austerity and discards all principles, destroys people's dreams, and does so whilst saying, "for the good of the company."

For the good of the company, don't start off stupid in the beginning, or fail to realize in the middle, when you are.

So How Do I Manage a Moral Business?

- It's *your* responsibility to lead by example.
- It's *your* responsibility to know what you're doing in the beginning so you don't get into trouble later on.
- It's *your* responsibility to tell everyone of the risk and reward associated with joining you in battle.
- It's *your* responsibility to:

    * Teach
    * Help
    * Support
    * Stabilize
    * Provide and enhance creativity
    * Provide moral confidence
    * Do unto others . . .

C.B.P. *Being a moral person in business is not necessarily a religious experience. It's about honesty, integrity, caring, commitment, and hope building.*

Start your company, build your company, or change your company to the "Moral Thing" and your chances of success will always be greatly enhanced.

C.B.P. The "Mean Business" approach is fundamental clarity to stupidity at the top.

"Do unto others" is never the wrong thing to do, and if your business fails, it won't be because you were not a good and decent person. It would have failed just the same if you applied the Mean Business approach. But at least you'll find the kind of person we all wish to hire and work with in the mirror every morning.

18

You Need Old Warhorses and Young Warriors

Did you ever wonder why you never see:

- A fifteen-year-old astronaut?
- A twenty-year-old general?
- A thirty-year-old world leader?
- An "In My Yuppie Prime" Pope?

Or ponder for a moment why:

- All junior accountants look like they're eighteen?
- Your mom will never be in a Calvin Klein commercial?
- Forty-year-old football players are only found in the park and hospitals on Sunday?
- Only your children can connect videogames to the TV?

Done wondering and pondering?

Real simple, ain't it? Any successful business needs a good mix of *old warhorses and young warriors.*

Why?

Old warhorses bring to the business years of experience at

failing. Young warriors bring to the business the arrogance and confidence to aggressively fail with great gusto.

Well, maybe that's a little harsh, but you must admit there is a great deal of truth to be found there.

Allow me to dig just a bit deeper:

C.B.P. There is no substitute for experience, and real experience can only be developed over time.

The most successful company in the industry where I spent most of my career got there by following this principle. I can recall in the early seventies when this highly regarded company's sales were less than $15 million annually. Now they exceed $1.5 billion. They have helped many of their employees to become wealthy people, and their stock has done phenomenally year after year.

For years, this company has recruited the brightest right out of college. Did they make them all VPs immediately? I think not. The program was to place them on the first rung of the ladder and carefully develop their potential. In addition to the philosophy of hiring the brightest, my vision of their program worked as follows:

- Recruit intelligent, educated, career-minded people.
- Start them at the point closest to the customer.
- Let them see the total ladder and instill the belief that it's yours to climb.
- Fast-track movement and opportunity.
- Quickly weed out those without the right stuff.
- Let them learn from those who have spent the time in grade to properly teach.
- Follow this process *every* year.

Now keep in mind, this company did not begin with a small group of bright kids right out of college. It began as a *family* business and with some pretty good warhorses at the top.

In the past twenty-five years, this organization has built a company that is *smart, driven,* and *aggressive* and has a perfect mix of: old warhorses and young warriors!

Now you may be just starting a business or developing one. And you could say, "Well, Steve, I can't afford to hire the college grad," or, "We're too small to have a formal training apparatus." Wrong!

C.B.P. The size and success of your company tomorrow will depend on the people you hire today.

It doesn't matter if you only have 2 employees or 200. If it's only 2, 1 of you must be the trainer and the other must be the trainee.

This organization did not go from a small, local company to the biggest and best in the industry overnight. They got there by preparing the team *today* for *tomorrow's* opportunity. I tell you this principle turned into practice will work every time.

One of my very favorite programs, and I'm proud to claim fame to its inception, has been the Replace Yourself Program.

In our business careers, whether as an owner, manager, or hourly employee, we all have faced the pressure of succeeding. Pressure to be better comes in three ways:

1. *Superior's pressure*—the boss says "Do it," "Do it now," "Do it my way," or "Hit the pavement."
2. *Peer pressure*—I am competing for the next promotion with the individual on the same organization chart line.
3. *Fire-down-below pressure*—I am smarter than my boss and one day I will be his boss.

I personally believe that fire-down-below pressure is the most effective. It challenges the subordinate to think about and reach for the rung above. At the same time, it forces the boss to stay on his toes and continuously strive for personal improvement.

With this in mind, I instructed *every manager* within the company and at every level to designate a subordinate as a potential replacement of their own position. If an appropriate candidate was not available, we transferred in or recruited new.

With my guidance and approval, a long-term training and development program was designed for every subordinate management employee. In many cases, the manager training his replacement also became the subordinate in training below his boss.

Did it work? Of course it did. I found it amazing how it improved teamwork and provided a healthy mental attitude among the management team. Instead of secretly attempting to take the boss's job, the boss was training the subordinate to accomplish it!

An added benefit derived from this program eliminated the dreaded fear of, "Gosh, I hope I never lose this manager; this person is critical." By developing replacements within the organization for every manager, I would never again be held hostage by someone who knew how badly he was needed.

As well, you will occasionally find that border-line individual who is just barely getting by. Without a readily available replacement, sometimes you have no choice but to live with a sub-par performer. As the old saying goes . . .

C.B.P. If you're stranded in the desert, don't ever shoot your camel, no matter how slow he is, until you find a new one to ride!

So how do I ensure that I'm developing the proper mix of old warhorses and young warriors?

If you've learned anything so far in this book, you now know how critical it is to have a short-term and long-term defined plan.

Step One: Develop an organization chart for one year, three years, and five years.

Step Two: Determine who the warhorses are and if they can sustain the pace throughout the five years. If the answer is no, allow them to be the horses that walk with the thoroughbreds to the gate *before* "AND THEY'RE OFF!"

Step Three: Find the young warriors within the organization and carefully analyze their ability and potential. Place them below and working for your best warhorses and chart their progress through the five-year organizational development, *with* a defined training program.

Step Four: If you are short in both horses and warriors now, begin the recruiting effort immediately.

Step Five: You must find the right mix of both, and you will most likely realize a five-to-one ratio of young warriors to old warhorses.

Step Six: The Replace Yourself Program doesn't end with the manager just below you. You must also select and develop *your replacement.*

The best CEO is one who has one.

—Malcolm Forbes

19
Why Most Businesses Fail

Obviously, there are a multitude of reasons that a business fails and too numerous to address. But there are only a handful of reasons that . . . *MOST* businesses fail!

1. Lack of cash
2. Wrong idea
3. Weak supporting cast
4. I crossed over the wall
5. Stupid management

I can proudly say and have earned the right to exhortation for no other reason than I have never failed at managing a business.

Allowing a brief moment of self-indulgence, I'll go further by proclaiming:

- I have managed forty-seven separate plants all across America.
- I have been responsible for 155 franchise operations, consisting mostly of small family entrepreneurs, in the United States, Canada, Mexico, Argentina, and New Zealand.
- I have achieved the position of COO for two public companies and CEO of one.
- I have started from scratch and developed a successful ad agency and janitorial business.

- I have been given partial ownership in a thriving, well-respected family business.
- I believed I had the audacity, self-important importance, and know-it-all ability to write this book and start my own consulting business.
- And last, I don't believe there has existed anyone with the diverse small-business experience I have accumulated and the matching ego to think someone would care enough to buy this book.

So, if you've read this far . . . I've proven myself right once again!

Well, thank you for listening to my profound horn blowing. Now, let's get back to how most businesses fail and what you can do to evade the toilet ride.

1. Lack of Cash

C.B.P. "*It takes money to make money*" *is not just a clever statement. It is an unequivocal truth.*

Far too many people start their business on a hope and a prayer, underfunded and unaware of some very basic business principles; i.e.,

- You start your business and most times optimistically forecast sales at 125 percent of reality.
- You fail to realize that your receivables will *begin* at forty-five days.
- Most vendors will start you on COD.
- Each employee will expect a paycheck the week he worked, not the week you collected receivables.
- Something will break and you will have a major expense not planned for.

- If you make money the first year, you are the exemplary example of chapter 17, *"The Moral Thing,"* and God loves you.

So How Do I Get beyond the First Toilet Ride?

- Forecast your sales at 75 percent of expectations the first year. It feels good to achieve in the beginning, and it forces you to live within a budget where costs have been planned for on a lower sales base.
- Your debt burden should not exceed 50 percent of your net bottom line cash during the first three years and less than that going forward.
- Plan for zero revenue the first sixty days relative to your cash requirements to operate the business.
- As quickly as possible and preferably on day one, have a thirty-day, all-operating-cash-requirements nest egg.
- Attempt to find *consignment* vendors wherever possible.
- Call *any* and every account that goes one day past thirty days current and offer a prompt pay discount to all charge customers.
- Budget and plan from the middle of best-case and worst-case scenarios.
- Understand and apply ROI standards to *everything* and everybody weekly.
- Be prepared to screw up and move on.
- Buy the book *101 Ways to Cook Spam*. (You might get hungry the first year!)

2. Wrong Idea

Many beginner entrepreneurs fail for no other reason than

what they thought was a good idea was in fact the wrong idea. Examples:

- I'm starting a computer business and my last three jobs were as an auto mechanic.
- I bought a franchise after listening to some well-dressed slick company representative who told me about just the success stories.
- I always wanted a restaurant, because I can grill the best steak in the neighborhood.
- If I open a bar, all my buddies will come.
- Daddy gave me the money.
- I've always been a hard worker, so who cares if I got a GED?

Sorry . . . I'll return to serious endeavors.

C.B.P. If you are going to start a new business or diversify an existing business, make sure you know the business well or employ someone that does.

C.B.P. The right idea with the wrong people is no different from the wrong idea with the right people.

How Do I Know It's the Right Idea?

- You have ample experience working for somebody else who has succeeded.
- *Many* have gone before you successfully.
- Your business plan is accepted by the bank.
- The risk is not greater than the reward.
- Failure will not destroy your existing business.
- Failure will not cause you to lose your house.

3. Weak Supporting Cast

This is probably one of the biggest problems for entrepreneurs. Why? Because many entrepreneurs believe they should be involved in every decision and every aspect of managing the business. With such overwhelming arrogance, they will most certainly:

- Fail to delegate, thus fail to develop, thus maintain a supporting cast of dummies.
- Run off anyone worth keeping.
- Never recruit based on potential long-term contribution ability, rather hire based on basic get-the-product-out needs today.

C.B.P. A business never runs by itself. People make it succeed or fail. Your business will be a mirrored reflection of your employment practices.

Too many times and too many businesspeople focus only on today's activity. If you are managing, own, or plan to own a business, the absolutely most critical asset you will need is a strong, smart supporting cast.

Let's take me as the example:

Steve Bryant's Strengths	Weaknesses
*Sales and marketing	*Administration
*Financial analyses	*H/R Compliance
*Training and Development	*Engineering

In the last company I managed as CEO, I hired *two* senior vice presidents: Pam Kelly, Administration and Human Relations Functions; and Nelson Masarjian, Engineering. Both forgot more about their jobs than I knew. By hiring a strong supporting cast that carried the management load of my weaknesses, I focused on the areas where I could be most productive.

Have you ever honestly and thoroughly evaluated yourself? There are many firms throughout the country that do that sort of thing.

Take the time and spend the money to find *your weaknesses*. Once you have been courageous enough to evaluate yourself, you will then recognize just where you will most likely screw up. That determined, hire, train, delegate those functions where you fall into the dummy category and focus on the areas where you can bring the greatest return.

4. I Crossed over the Wall

I like to think of myself as a man's man. You know, ex-marine, got my Black Belt at the age of forty-six, never met a challenge I didn't like, and rarely find it necessary to admit any mistake. But with all that bravado . . . the wall always frightened me.

What is the wall, you ask? That barrier that secretly hides failure, financial ruin, and the reality of cannot return. And you know that wall is ever present in both our business and personal lives. It looms out there in the darkness just barely within our sight, calling salaciously, "Come play with us forever!"

We've all been tempted by the wall. That one big roll of the dice. The big score. The chance of a lifetime. I have been to Las Vegas a hundred times, and I have never come home with more than I started with.

The wall is the big make-or-break decision. The wall is go for broke.

Always remember, your main goal in the beginning was to create a secure, growing, profitable business. Never forget or lose that focus, and stay away from the wall.

5. Stupid Management

Yes, folks, you are right. You have hit the jackpot . . . COME ON DOWN!

The number-one reason businesses fail is: *STUPID MANAGEMENT.*

Think about it:

- Who started the business without a clue of the necessary cash requirements?
- Who began, stayed with, and tried to force the wrong idea?
- Who failed to recruit, hire, and train the right people, leaving the company with a weak supporting cast?
- Who crossed over the wall, devastating and destroying the existing business?

Who? You got it . . . the STUPID MANAGER.

As someone very wise once said: "Even a fool doesn't wish to follow a fool."

How can I avoid the stupid manager syndrome?

Well, you've made a really good start by purchasing my book. Now all you have to do is apply it chapter by chapter.

C.B.P. Stupid managers don't just suddenly appear. They are created.

I guess it goes back to the Peter Principle, and a very sound principle it is. Eventually, if one continues to be promoted, he will someday reach his own level of incompetence.

On numerous occasions I have witnessed excellent, bright, and successful managers wake up to stupid after the last promotion. But they can find a cure, and it is called *overcompensation.*

That you are not the smartest guy in the world is indeed a fact. You are not the best person in the company for every job. Therefore, you must surround yourself with talent and know-how. That will automatically make you a *very smart manager.*

C.B.P. If you are wearing several hats in managing your business, it only means you have a very large head, most likely helium-endowed.

20
The Three Ps

This will be a very brief chapter, but not diminished in importance. After careful review, if you will apply this chapter's message, I will guarantee you can add three full percentage points to your bottom line.

The three Ps:
- People
- Pricing
- Productivity

People

Throughout this book I have reiterated many times that your most important asset is your people. Bad employees can only exist because of two reasons:

1. You hired them already bad.
2. You made them bad.

I can honestly say that of the thousands of employees I have worked with in the past thirty years, I cannot think of ten who would be considered worthless.

We too often fail to realize that every employee is just like you and me. They have bills, problems, worries, kids, and a job. A lot of times we can't always help them with their financial situation, solve their problems, eliminate their worries, or raise their children. We can, however, make their job more rewarding.

Think about this: Your job is to manage twenty people. How much time and effort would it take to commit to knowing them better? Let's say you decide to spend *two hours* with each employee and discuss what's important to them. Get to know what inspires them, what causes them to have hope. Then study their jobs and the surrounding work environments. Put yourself in their jobs and think about what you would enjoy, how to inject a little fun into it. Spend a careful four, totally dedicated, hours to this endeavor. Then for each employee bring the employee back to the discussion with your conclusions and solicit his feedback. All that's left to implement are the positive changes.

You have now spent eight hours or a total of four weeks with one of your most important and necessary assets, the people who help run your company. Will it be worth the time? You're darn right it will be!

In my particular industry, labor cost averaged 35 percent of total revenue. If I improve productivity by *3 percent,* I add one additional point to my bottom line.

If your business generates 80 percent full productivity from your employees, you are doing well. Now you tell me if a dedicated and involved effort in making their jobs better won't improve their desire and commitment. The increased desire and commitment translates into increased productivity, which equates with increased profit! You need another one point to the bottom line? Ask your employees . . . they *want to do it!*

Pricing

I've never seen a business that could not raise their prices 1 percent any time they so desired and do so without customer resistance. As well, if you'll carefully and regularly review each customer invoice, you will, I guarantee, find more pricing mistakes in the customers' favor than in your own. I'll further declare that these errors when corrected will add a half-point to your bottom line.

Do both every six months and stay ahead of inflation and supplier increases. Your normal price-increasing activity will go straight to the bottom-line contribution.

Productivity

Remember chapter 1, *"What Gets Measured Gets Managed!"*

Stop for a moment; clear your head; get your legal pad and pencil ready. Now write down every single thing you measure *carefully* each week. Done? Good. Now write down everything in your business that can and should be measured. Throw away the first list and begin developing the systems to accurately and frequently measure the second list.

There is nothing in your business that doesn't present the opportunity to measure it. Let me also say that I have never found anything in business that, when properly measured, could not adapt easily into the management of that measurement and improve 100 percent of the time.

I learned a long time ago . . .

C.B.P. It takes 100 pennies to make a dollar. Penny managers always do better than dollar managers."

21

The Ten Steve Bryant Country Boy Business Principles

The following ten principles were developed for a corporate presentation before the board of directors and U.S. Division company presidents for the Johnson Group PLC. The purpose of the presentation was for Steve Bryant to explain how he had successfully turned around three failing companies within the corporation. Thus the Country Boy Principles were born.

1. The Only True Measurement of Ability Is Results. —*Malcolm Forbes*

- Degrees on the office wall only indicate that you successfully attended school.
- P&L statements indicate that you can successfully manage a business.
- It doesn't matter how smart *you* think you are, and it doesn't matter how smart *others* think you are. All that matters in business and life is . . . *Can You Walk the Talk?*

2. Battle Plans Win and Lose Wars

Development of a successful battle plan:

- Get down and dirty in the trench review of the front lines. (You better know as much as the troops.)
- Know the goal, and ensure it's realistic. Be a hero at the end, not the beginning. BS applies to Blue Skiers, too.
- Develop a buy-in attitude. Nobody makes your numbers long-term. They must have input.
- Document, agree, and assign responsibility.
- Overmanage the beginning stages of plan implementation.
- Practice minimal but precise activity and performance reporting. The focus ain't in the reporting; it's in the doing.
- Plans developed, *accept nothing less.* No plan works 100 percent, so be prepared to: *ADAPT, IMPROVISE,* and *OVERCOME.*

3. We Don't Promise You a Rose Garden

- Never tell your troops you are all going to a parade and then drop napalm on them. If it's going to be tough, everyone needs to know upfront.
- Any major turnaround needs one heck of a lot more grunts than it needs general officers.

Find the Warriors at Every Level

- Weed out the sissies and crybabies quickly.
- Clearly explain the battle plan and the toughness necessary to win. (*Most* people hate losing and will fight with you if they know what they're fighting for.)
- Always tell your people the truth. If you need eighty hours a week, tell them.

- Set the example. Just because a business card lists a title doesn't automatically make anyone a leader.

4. The Avis Theory

- Shop at home first. Understand that 50 percent of the time hiring from the outside means inheriting somebody else's problems.
- It takes a lot of time and money to recruit and train new managers. Most turnarounds, which was the case in every job I've had, should take months, not years. *It is the exception, not the rule,* when a new manager contributes significantly *in a turnaround* situation. If your company's doing fine, this is not the case.
- Avis Theory: Any time you have an important opening, look around at the people you have. If you think someone has 50 percent of what you need, give him a shot. Ninety-five percent of the time he will succeed.
- The pipeline starts at the beginning of the drill, not at the refinery.

5. Lean and Mean

- Corporate offices exist for one reason only, *Support to Operations.*
- The fewer people at the top, the less nonrevenue, nonprofit paperwork in the field.
- Don't add staff until operations can afford to pay for them.
- Every employee on staff should have a measurable top-line or bottom-line responsibility.
- Without clear line authority, staff people are basically wasting their time.

- Ultimate rule—put people dollars at the closest possible point to the customer.

6. The Bottom Line Is Top-Line

- The CEO of any organization should spend 50 percent of his time focusing on top-line development.
- Strong sales hide most sins—declining sales expose them.
- In any turnaround, the focus should be:

    1. Improved service *and* sales development
    2. Improved quality *and* sales development
    3. Improved cost control *and* sales development

If you set your battle plan to accomplish 1–3 before a strong focus on top-line, you might not make it to sales development.
- Customers will pay more for quality and service.
- You should spend more money on marketing and sales development than you do on administrative overhead.

7. Take No Prisoners

- Never be controlled by what your competitors are doing, *but* always be keenly aware of their activity.
- Never blame lack of performance on competition.
- Never let the opponent define you or the fight.
- Understand that market share can sometimes be as bad as it is good.
- Watch and monitor closely the success and failures of the industry. (You can always tell the pioneers by the arrows in their backs.)

8. ROI Applies to People, Too

- No *one* in any organization should feel like they are not responsible for something tangible.
- Do ROIs on people *before* hiring them.
- Good firing ability is every bit as important as good hiring ability (one shot, one kill).
- *Productivity incentives work;* use them often, top to bottom.
- ROI every manager or staff person. It might scare you.
- Compensation is not intangible, so neither should the results be.

9. It's Cash, Stupid

- Entrepreneur and owner are not titles; *they are philosophies.* Instill that, *you win.*
- Overmanage accounts payable and payroll.
- Never buy new equipment if good used is available.
- The CEO should approve all accounts payable on a regular basis.
- Don't let depreciation appreciate.

10. Expect to Win

- All battle plans and goals need a reason to rally.
- Clearly present the *single theme* to all employees and constantly reinforce it.
- Don't ever project a slogan that you yourself are not adamantly committed to.
- Challenges, camaraderie, and blood, sweat, and tears need a call to arms.

- Cute doesn't cut it, tough does, so say it with fire.
- If you truly expect to win and sincerely instill that in your people, *you cannot fail.*

Winning is not a sometime thing; it's an all the time thing. You don't win once in a while; you don't do things right once in a while; you do them right all the time. Winning is a habit. Unfortunately, so is losing.

—Vince Lombardi

22
One-liners with a Punch

Losing the fight is not nearly as painful if you lose it with integrity.

You can never overmanage the numbers, but you should not attempt to micromanage the numbers, either.

Monday morning quarterbacks never win the game.

Generally speaking, if you wait until someone pulls the trigger before you measure how close you are, you will most likely get shot.

Lazy sales reps make hungry owners.

Always be aware of what your competition is doing, but never be controlled by it.

Every business that begins with the correct detailed profit-driven pricing structure . . . eventually ends there as well . . . profitably.

If you don't know how to do it and it's of major importance, most likely hiring someone with the necessary talent is a wise decision. Good people never cost you money.

If you have cattle to rustle, hire a cowboy, not an MBA consultant!

Reward, advancement, and leadership responsibility should only go to the individual who puts money in your pocket rather than accolades in your ear.

Show me first. Tell me after.

A growing business needs action people, not study hall monitors.

How many really creative administrators have you ever known?

Quality can be as much perception as reality.

Do it good first . . . fast second.

You should never lose a customer to poor quality.

Short-term goal achievement will always chase down long-term goal reality.

Catchup is a dirty word and usually the medal worn by the loser.

If you overachieve early . . . you'll continue to overachieve.

Be a sprinter, even if the race is a minimarathon. I'd much prefer being tired and chased to having lots of energy and running last.

Morality isn't just for Sundays.

The good things you do from your heart for people will always come back . . . and so will the bad things.

The quality of the people hired today will drive the company's success for tomorrow.

If an employee fails to reach his maximum realistic potential, 80 percent of the time it is because you failed to develop him.

ROI applies to everything in business and generally is associated with hard assets. But always remember that people are the greatest asset and *everybody has a bottom line.* Find it, develop it, and reward it!

Owners', stockholders'; and investors' greed is the reason for many businesses taking the toilet ride.

Any key employee who does not generate in new net cash double his compensation *every year* is not a true key employee.

Cost-of-living raises suck! Pay for achievement without a doesn't-make-sense cap.

Key employees make your bottom line happen. *You* must find their bottom line and make it happen when *yours* has been realized.

You can never overpay a key employee if investors are smiling.

Everybody has a bottom line. The further down the organization you reach and realize, the stronger your company will become.

Your competitors will steal all your "Mr. Jones" customers and you will continue to sell to the "Hey, Charlies"!

A company that responds to each customer as if he were the *only customer* will almost always keep that customer.

When you get so big and important that a customer's call can wait, prepare to add additional salespeople.

Busy and productive don't always walk down the same street hand in hand.

A minute wasted could be a dollar lost.

If you are not consistently well organized, your business will become disorganized and your employees will become mirror watchers . . . and it will be your mirror they are looking into.

The first generation starts the business. The second generation builds the business. The third generation screws it up!

You can't swim in quicksand.

Usually when the smoke clears, you'll find someone got burnt.

When it appears to be too good to be true . . . it most often is.

It's easier to spot a wolf in sheep's clothing than to recognize a beagle dressed like a rabbit.

If you sell your business and get enough for it to do everything else in life you wish to do, it is a no-brainer.

We are buying your business, and nothing is going to change.

I've Got a Secret was an old television show, not a legitimate approach for selling your business.

Timing is everything, or so they say. But right timing with no money is boredom the hard way.

For entrepreneurs, the *ability* for adaptation practice is too often a lesson learned after the fact.

Improvisation is a God-given talent like music or painting. It's not a college course, but it can be learned, if practiced.

The ability to *adapt* and *improvise* will always allow you to *overcome* the obstacle.

There is always more than one tree in any forest.

Without the ability to *adapt, improvise,* and *overcome,* you will never have the opportunity to maximize the opportunity.

Fear for one's job will never develop love for the owner's goals.

"Mean Business" practices have never in the history of the world started as the beginning of the process. They are always, 100 percent of the time, at the end of all activity.

Austerity programs are easily defined as the people at the top screwed up.

Austerity programs today, prosperity tomorrow, bought out eventually.

Being a moral person in business is not necessarily a religious experience. It's about honesty, integrity, caring, commitment, and hope building.

The "Mean Business" approach is fundamental clarity to stupidity at the top.

There is no substitute for experience and real experience can only be developed in time.

The size and success of your company tomorrow will depend on the people you hire today.

If you're stranded in the desert, don't ever shoot your camel, no matter how slow he is, until you find a new one to ride!

"It takes money to make money" is not just a clever statement. It is an unequivocal truth.

If you are going to start a new business or diversify an existing business, make sure you know the business well, or employ someone who does.

The right idea with the wrong people is no different from the wrong idea with the right people.

A business never runs by itself. People make it succeed or fail. Your business will be a mirrored reflection of your employment practices.

Stupid managers don't just suddenly appear. They are created.

If you are wearing several hats in managing your business, it only means you have a very large head, most likely helium-endowed.

It takes 100 pennies to make a dollar. Penny managers always do better than dollar managers.

23
Conclusion

I am extremely proud that I finally seized the initiative to put pen to paper and share the concepts and practices that took this dumb old county boy from grocery clerk to CEO. I hope within the pages of this book you will find just one idea that will stop a mistake from occurring, one system that will dramatically improve your bottom line, or a single principle that will increase your chance of success. If you apply the lessons taught, something good will happen.

You must, however, make a conscious decision at this moment in time. Moving forward, will you be a busy manager or a focused manager? Will you lead or dictate? Will you succeed or fail?

Read the book; think about it. Then begin with chapter 1 and implement. I can promise you at the end you will be a much improved manager and your business will have dramatically increased bottom-line results.

After all, my friend, the reason you are in business to begin with is, in fact, identical to the reason I wrote this book: **FOR THE MONEY!**